The Millennial Collection

Sandra J. Berbeco

Friends of the Newton Free Library

SYRACUSE BASKETBALL: A CENTURY OF MEMORIES

FROM THE ARCHIVES OF
THE SYRACUSE NEWSPAPERS

www.sportspublishinginc.com

THE SYRACUSE NEWSPAPERS

STEPHEN A. ROGERS, EDITOR AND PUBLISHER
MICHAEL CONNOR, EXECUTIVE EDITOR
STAN LINHORST, SENIOR MANAGING EDITOR
STEVE CARLIC, SPORTS EDITOR
JIM KLEINKLAUS, ADVERTISING AND MARKETING DIRECTOR

THE REPRINTED ARTICLES AND PHOTOGRAPHS WERE ORIGINALLY PUBLISHED IN
THE SYRACUSE NEWSPAPERS. IN SOME INSTANCES, ARTICLES APPEARING IN THIS BOOK
HAVE BEEN EDITED TO ACCOMMODATE CERTAIN SPACE LIMITATIONS. HOWEVER,
WHEREVER POSSIBLE, WE HAVE INCLUDED THE ARTICLES IN THEIR ENTIRETY.

COORDINATING EDITOR: BOB SNYDER
DEVELOPMENTAL EDITORS: THOMAS H. BAST AND
VICTORIA J. MARINI
BOOK DESIGN, PROJECT MANAGER: JENNIFER L. POLSON
DUSTJACKET AND INSERT DESIGN: JULIE L. DENZER AND
TERRY NEUTZ HAYDEN

ISBN: 1-58382-107-5
LIBRARY OF CONGRESS CATALOG CARD NUMBER: 99-68622

PRINTED IN THE UNITED STATES OF AMERICA.

SPORTS PUBLISHING INC.
804 NORTH NEIL STREET
CHAMPAIGN, ILLINOIS 61820
WWW.SPORTSPUBLISHINGINC.COM

ACKNOWLEDGMENTS

COMPILING THE GREATEST MOMENTS IN *SYRACUSE BASKETBALL HISTORY* REQUIRED THE HELPING HANDS OF NUMEROUS INDIVIDUALS IN THE NEWSROOM OF THE SYRACUSE NEWSPAPERS.

WE HAD THE SUPPORT OF EDITOR AND PUBLISHER STEVE ROGERS AND MIKE CONNOR, THE PAPER'S EXECUTIVE EDITOR.

PARTICULAR THANKS TO HARRY DiORIO, THE PAPER'S DIRECTOR OF PHOTOGRAPHY, AND MANY OF HIS FINE STAFF MEMBERS FOR GOING ABOVE AND BEYOND THE CALL OF DUTY TO PROVIDE SHOTS THAT ILLUSTRATE SO MANY MEMORABLE MOMENTS. ALSO, THANKS TO EVERYONE IN THE LIBRARY WHO ASSISTED IN OUR COMBING THROUGH ARCHIVES AND VIEWING HUNDREDS OF REELS OF MICROFILM.

AND, OF COURSE, TO MARSHA AND OUR LESLEY, FOR ENCOURAGING ME DURING THE PROJECT.

BOB SNYDER
COORDINATING EDITOR

JOHN BERRY, THE SYRACUSE NEWSPAPERS

A RECORD CROWD OF 33,015 GATHERS AT THE CARRIER DOME AS SU TAKES ON GEORGETOWN IN THE 1989-90 SEASON.

CONTENTS

A Pictorial Retrospective

Ed Stickel makes an airborne shot for two of his 38 points in a 1949 victory over Canisius at the State Fair Coliseum.

THE SYRACUSE NEWSPAPERS

Mᴀʀᴋ Wᴀʟᴅᴀᴄʜ (30) ᴀɴᴅ ᴀɴ ᴏᴘᴘᴏɴᴇɴᴛ ʜᴀɴɢ ɪɴ ꜱᴜꜱᴘᴇɴᴅᴇᴅ ᴀɴɪᴍᴀᴛɪᴏɴ.

Bɪʟʟ Sᴍɪᴛʜ ɢᴏᴇꜱ ꜰᴏʀ ᴀ ʙʟᴏᴄᴋᴇᴅ ꜱʜᴏᴛ ᴠꜱ. Pᴇɴɴ'ꜱ Pʜɪʟ Hᴀɴᴋɪɴꜱᴏɴ.

P EARL WASHINGTON'S SHOT IS BLOCKED BY NAVY'S DAVID ROBINSON IN SU'S NCAA LOSS IN THE CARRIER DOME.

E RICH SANTIFER JUMPS OUT ON BRYAN WARRICK, BUT ST. JOE'S PLAYS BEAT THE CLOCK AND DEFEATS SU IN THE 1981 CARRIER CLASSIC FINAL.

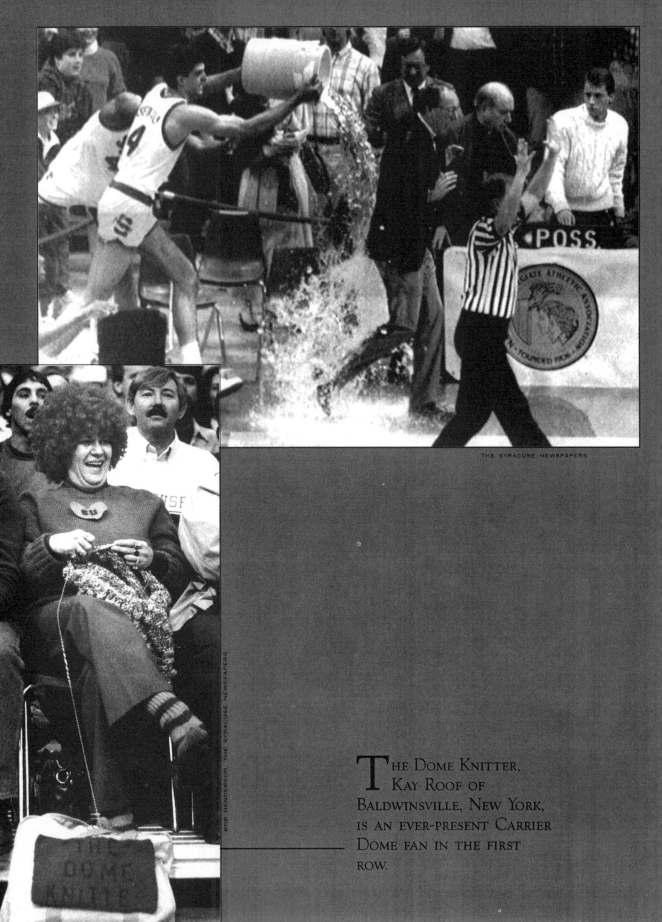

Rony Seikaly puts coach Jim Boeheim on ice during the Road to the Final Four in 1987.

THE SYRACUSE NEWSPAPERS

BOB HENDERSON, THE SYRACUSE NEWSPAPERS

The Dome Knitter, Kay Roof of Baldwinsville, New York, is an ever-present Carrier Dome fan in the first row.

DERRICK COLEMAN GOES HIGH ABOVE THE REST AND USES TWO HANDS
TO JAM HOME TWO POINTS AS VILLANOVA DEFENDERS LOOK ON IN 1988.

SYRACUSE FANS WELCOME HOME THE
BASKETBALL TEAM AT MANLEY
FIELDHOUSE AFTER SU LOST TO INDIANA
74-73 FOR THE NCAA TITLE.

Dave Bing, considered by many to be SU's greatest player, is enshrined in Basketball's Hall of Fame in 1990.

Billy Owens drives past Georgetown's Alonzo Mourning.

FOREWORD

BY JIM BOEHEIM

A generation younger than my own has seen us only in our Carrier Dome home. But, of course, Syracuse basketball began long before we began playing basketball under a Teflon bubble . . . before I walked on the Hill, a kid from nearby Lyons with dreams of playing big-time college hoops.

Even before Bob Snyder—having matriculated here and, he tells me, gaining a degree—began covering the US beat.

Now, he's compiled a century of stories and columns appearing in The Syracuse Newspapers, some his own, tracing 100 years of US basketball and the exploits of those who wrote court history.

From Vic Hanson to the Reindeer Five . . . Bullet Billy Gabor to Dave Bing, my roomie and the greatest to ever play the game at SU . . . Sweet D and the Brothers Lee . . . Roy's Runts . . . Divine Providence and California, Here We Come! (SU's first trip to the Final Four) . . . Bouie 'n Louie . . . The Pearl and Derrick Coleman . . . National Championship games with Indiana and Kentucky.

For me, it's been a magic carpet ride, a 37-year journey that began the first time I ever laced 'em up to step foot on the court with Bing.

Syracuse Basketball: A Century of Memories chronicles all that and more. Not just the best of times, of which there have been many, but moments of dejection, not the least of which was probation, which touches most programs. We paid the price, particularly in recruiting, and moved on.

We've always moved on. From the worst team in America—well, it lost what was then an NCAA-record 27 consecutive games—Syracuse rose from the basketball junk heap when Fred Lewis, my coach, came and brought Bing with him. Four years later, we were playing for the NCAA East Regional crown.

Hopefully, you learn from a Lewis . . . from a Roy Danforth, my boss when we made it to the '75 Final Four won by a retiring John Wooden.

You learn in victory, and certainly in defeat. And it's never easy to forget the latter; it shouldn't be. That's why they keep score.

The toughest loss I ever endured on the court was a high school championship game. And that was m-m-m-m-m years ago.

Every program has its down time. But throughout the history of Syracuse basketball, one of the winningest in the country, a hallmark has been consistency.

You have to go back more than 30 years, to the '60s, when we had a losing season.

That's a tribute to the kids who've played the game . . . the heralded All-Americans and those not heavily pursued, who made themselves better and took the program to greater heights . . . and to our fans.

The Syracuse faithful have trudged through snow and sleet in unparalleled number. No college basketball program has received the support we've had—setting NCAA turnstile records and leading the nation at the gate year after year for more than a decade.

If they're demanding, well, they should be. They've always wanted for us no less than we wanted ourselves.

Success.

They span the generation gap, our fans do. From days preceding the Manley Dome, where I played and first coached . . . dust from a practice football field rising from beneath an elevated wooden floor . . . The Manley Zoo creating a crescendo of sound that made it a tough place for visitors to play.

They were with us every step of the way, from a program with a regional reputation to one recognized coast to coast as a perennial 20-game winner/NCAA Tournament team.

Sure, we'd love to win the ultimate game. And some Monday night, some year, perhaps we will. We've been close before.

Hopefully, we'll be there again. Great players, great kids, great fans can combine to make it happen.

In the meantime, enjoy *Syracuse Basketball: A Century of Memories*—a 100-year chronicle from days of the center jump to the alley-oop . . . from the beginning of a century to the brink of a new millennium.

Go George!

—*Jim Boeheim*
Syracuse basketball coach

SYRACUSE GUARD DAVE BING CONCENTRATES WHILE PRACTICING FREE THROWS.

BASKETBALL TEAM TO PLAY

VARSITY FIVE MEETS R.P.I. TEAM
AT SCHENECTADY TONIGHT

JANUARY 5, 1901 | BY TOM O'DONNELL, SYRACUSE HERALD

The Syracuse University basketball team will meet the Rensselaer Polytechnic Institute team at Schenectady tonight in the intercollegiate series. The local team will leave for Schenectady at 12:35 today.

It will be the first game of the season for the local basketball team, and the result will be watched with much interest by the students and Athletic Committee on the hill. The team has practiced diligently for the past several weeks, and it is expected that a good showing will be made.

The team will be chosen from the following who will go: Gannett, Twomble, Goodwin, Lamb, Low and Whittemore. Captain Hansel will not play, as he has been ill for the past two weeks and is out of condition.

Next week Cornell will be played in this city and January 23 the Yale team will be met in the gymnasium on the hill. It will be the first appearance of a blue team in Syracuse for many years. During February the team will make a trip through New England.

E.R. Sweetland was yesterday morning named as coach of the University crew for another season. He began work yesterday afternoon, when 18 freshman candidates reported in the gymnasium and were put through light preliminary practice on the machines. The work will be continued daily until the races in June. It is planned to keep a larger number of men in training this year than was the case last. The work on Onondaga Lake is also expected to begin earlier.

First Game Ever Syracuse Basketball Team Lost
| j a n u a r y 6, 1 9 0 1

The Rensselaer Polytechnic basketball team of Troy last evening defeated Syracuse University by a score of 21 to 8 at the State Armory in this city.

Colgate Beaten in Overtime Game by Orange Five

FEBRUARY 10, 1914 | FROM THE SYRACUSE HERALD

Hamilton, New York—Colgate lost to Syracuse at basketball in one of the closest and fastest games ever seen on the local gymnasium court. The score was 29 to 28, and it required two extra periods to decide the contest.

Syracuse played rings around Colgate in the first half, the Maroons scoring only five points, all of which were made by Kennedy on a basket and three fouls. In the second half, Bourne and Stewart were sent in for Colgate, and the team took a remarkable brace. They put up the best exhibition of basketball this season, and far outplayed the Syracuse contingent in that half. Just before the whistle blew, Benzoni made a basket and tied the score, 26 to 26. An extra period of five minutes was played with no score by either team. In the second extra period, Syracuse shot a foul and made a basket, while Stewart made another for the Maroons. The play was not around the Syracuse goal when the bell rang. The referee turned toward the timekeepers and blew his whistle, turning back just in time to see the ball fall into the basket from Stewart's hands, but the contest was over before the ball was thrown, according to the timekeepers. Castle starred for Syracuse, making a total of fifteen points. Both teams were excellent defensively.

game summary | february 9, 1914

SYRACUSE (29)	COLGATE (28)
Notman	Kennedy, Stewart
Keib	Sefton, Bourne
Forwards	
Castle	Knapp, Johnson
Center	
Seymour	Huntington
Crisp, Decker	Benzoni
Guards	

Field baskets—Notman, 2; Castle, 6; Seymour, 1; Crisp, 2; Keib, 1; Decker, 1; Kennedy, 1; Benzoni, 4; Johnson, 1; Bourne, 3; Stewart, 1. Baskets from fouls—Castle, 3; Kennedy, 5; Bourne, 2; Stewart, 3. Referee—Hogan

statistics

ORANGE ENDS ITS BASKETBALL YEAR BY BEATING GREEN

MARCH 12, 1914 | FROM THE SYRACUSE HERALD

The Syracuse University basketball team closed the most successful season in the history of the sport here with a victory over Dartmouth last night. Outplaying their opponents at every stage of the game, Syracuse romped away with a 29 to 18 score. The game was slow and uninteresting to the spectators throughout.

Had the Orange played anything like they did in the Princeton or Pennsylvania contests they would have swamped the Green. During the first half the pass work was ragged, and Syracuse lost many easy chances to score. Nevertheless, Syracuse ran up a one-sided score in the first period that enabled them to loaf through the remainder of the contest.

Notman carried off the honors in scoring. In the first few minutes of play, "Dutch" caged the ball twice for the initial counts of the evening. He scored one more in this period, and in the second session tallied twice, making a total of 10 points for the game. Captain Castle was second in the order of scoring with one field and seven foul goals. Seymour netted the ball for four field goals, and Crisp furnished his usual pair of spectacular shots.

The contest was rather a disappointment to the large crowd of fans. Dartmouth had a team that weighed about the same as Syracuse, but they had little more than a fairly good system of passing to depend upon. Pelletier was forced to leave the floor because of four personal fouls. Captain Louden got two goals, which was as many as any member of that team secured, and played a good defensive game. Rector at center was a good jumper at the touch-off, but couldn't keep up with Castle in getting around the floor.

With the possible exception of the Notre Dame contest, no game that has been played here this year was so apparently lost to a team from the very beginning as was the case with Darmouth last night. Probably the long string of defeats that the Hanover team has experienced this season had sucked the vitality out of them, for they showed no semblance of fight at any time. It was easily the poorest exhibition that has been put in by any of the Intercollegiate League teams.

Syracuse has scored a total of 369 points for the season as compared to 214 for their opponents. Captain Castle led all the men in individual scoring with a total of 155 points. Notman was the second highest scorer with 68. As a general rule, the Orange did not run up such a high score against the easier opponents as is generally the case. On the other hand, they won all but two of the games by a comfortable margin. The Pittsburgh game here and the Colgate game at Hamilton were the closest contests, and both of these went into extra periods.

Captain Castle, Seymour and Notman played their last games for the Orange last night. All three had been valuable men for the last two seasons and will be greatly missed when it comes time to start on another campaign next year. Only Crisp and Kelb remain as a nucleus for the 1915 team.

SU's 1914 BASKETBALL TEAM. 1914 HELMS FOUNDATION ALL-AMERICAN LEW CASTLE IS SEATED IN THE MIDDLE, HOLDING THE BALL.

game summary | march 11, 1914

SYRACUSE (29)   **DARTMOUTH (18)**

Notman .... Whitney, Brownell
                    Left Forward
Keib .... Winship
                    Right Forward
Castle .... Rector
                    Center
Crisp .... Pelletier, Bickford
                    Left Guard
Seymour .... Louden
                    Right Guard

Goals from field—Syracuse: Notman 5, Seymour 4, Crisp 2, Castle 1; Dartmouth: Pelletier 2, Louden 2, Whitney 1, Brownell 1, Bickford 1. Goals from foul—Castle 5 out of 8 tries, Winship 2 out of 6 tries. Time of halves—20 minutes. Referee—Steinberg. Umpire—Marshall. Timer—Prof. W. C. Lowe.

statistics

19

ORANGE FIVE TO TACKLE QUINTET OF TROY TONIGHT

SYRACUSANS DOWN PENN 27 TO 24 AFTER HARD FIGHT

JANUARY 26, 1918 | FROM THE SYRACUSE HERALD

Philadelphia—Following their great victory over the University of Pennsylvania last night, the Syracuse University basketball team left for Troy where a game will be staged this evening with the Rensselaer Polytechnic Institute quintet.

Last night's battle between Syracuse and Penn is one that will not soon be forgotten. It was one of the most bitterly fought contests ever seen in this city, and every player on both teams battling as though his life depended on it. It was a bitter pill for the Quakers to swallow and they died hard, the score being 27 to 24. That Lon Jourdet's champion five, the leaders of the Intercollegiate League, should be routed on their own court was something that fairly amazed the crowd of basketball fans who witnessed the game.

Charles Dolley, the agile right forward of the Orange Five, is regarded here today as the circus tumbler of basketball. That contortionist stuff he got away with one might expect to see in the sawdust arena of a circus tent instead of in the black market arena of a basketball court. About every time Dolley slipped the ball into the air it settled within the meshes of the goal, no matter from what part of the court it was tossed and no matter in what position the Orange star was standing. Dolley had a total of five goals.

game summary | january 25, 1918

SYRACUSE (27)	PENNSYLVANIA (24)
J. Cronauer, lf.	rg., Peck
Dolley, rf.	lg., Mitchell
Schwarzer, c.	c., Davis
Marcus, lg.	rf., Stannard
Barsha, rg.	lf., Sweeney

Field goals Dolley, 5; J. Cronauer, 3; Schwarzer, 3; Romanot, 2; Sweeney 2; Davis, 2; Peck. Foul goals—Sweeney 10 out of 13; Schwarzer, 5 our of 13, Substitutions—Romanot for Stannard, Cronauer for Barsha. Referee—Tom Thorp. Umpire—George Cartwright. Time of halves —20 minutes.

statistics

Syracuse and Penn Will Have to Share Honors as 1918 Basketball Leaders

MARCH 16, 1918 | FROM THE SYRACUSE HERALD

The basketball quintets of Syracuse University and the University of Pennsylvania will have to share the honors of being the best basketball teams in the East this season as a result of the 17-to-16 victory of the Quakers over the Orange band in Archbold Gymnasium last night. Earlier in the season, the Syracusans trimmed the Pennsylvanians, 27 to 24, at Philadelphia, and last night the Quakers came here for revenge and got it. Twenty-five hundred persons were crowded about the court to see the basket tossers play the most important game ever staged in this city.

It was through the accurate shooting of Mike Sweeney, a sophomore from Atlantic City, who is playing his first year of basketball for the Quakers, that the visitors broke the winning streak of Eddie Dollard's five. Fourteen fouls were called on Syracuse by the officials, referee Tom Thorp of Columbia and Carl Reed of Springfield Training school, and out of that number of trials from the 15-foot mark, Sweeney dropped the ball through the netting 13 times. The other four points made by the victors were near the end of the first half, and Peck dropping the ball through the cage early in the last period.

Syracuse secured five field goals, every regular player on the quintet getting a basket, but when it came to shooting fouls, Syracuse was out of

THE SYRACUSE 1917-18 TEAM WAS THE HELMS FOUNDATION NATIONAL CHAMPS. PICTURED ARE CAPTAIN JOE SCHWARZER (WITH BALL) AND COACH EDDIE DOLLARD (BACK ROW, THIRD FROM LEFT).

the running. In all, fourteen fouls were called on Penn and but six points were registered from them. Capt. Joe Schwarzer was off color in shooting from the foul mark, making but five out of thirteen tries. Paul, a youngster who went into the game when Schwarzer was forced to leave the floor because of four personal fouls that had been called on him, had one chance to shoot a foul goal and he succeeded in caging the ball.

MARCH 16, 1918.

The contest was exceptionally fast and a bit rough at times. The players of both teams fought as if their very lives depended upon the outcome of the struggle. And while on the subject of fighting it may be well to mention here that Charley Dolley, the right forward of the Syracuse team, showed as much scrap as any player on the court. He was sent into the game to watch Captain Martin, the clever guard of the Penn team, and Dolley did so well that Martin never had a chance to shoot at a basket from inside the foul line. Dolley played the Quaker leader so hard that the latter was nearly exhausted near the finish.

From the Syracuse Herald

No Third Game Between Syracuse and Penn Fives
| m a r c h   2 1 ,   1 9 1 8

There will be no third game of basketball between the quintets of Syracuse University and the University of Pennsylvania for the college championship as the athletic authorities of Pennsylvania have refused to sanction a contest. An effort was made to have a third game staged in New York with the proceeds to be given to the Red Cross or to supply tobacco for soldiers across the big pond, but the plan fell through when the Pennsylvania authorities announced that the team had disbanded for the season.

Syracuse would have been willing to play a game for the Red Cross.

Hanson Shines as Orange Halts Quaker Strike

Scores 25 Points in Syracuse 30-25 Basketball Victory

DECEMBER 30, 1925 | FROM THE SYRACUSE HERALD

With Capt. Vic Hanson displaying basketball skill such as never before has been seen on Archbold gymnasium court, the Syracuse University basketball team nosed out the University of Pennsylvania five in an extra-period game last night, 30 to 25, the teams being deadlocked at 22, all at the end of the second half. Hanson equalled the total Penn score by tossing in eight field goals and nine foul goals for 25 points. It was the first defeat of the season for Penn.

Despite the fact that Hanson's greatest liking is for baseball and that he has been hailed as All-American football calibre, the exhibition he put up last night crowns him as one of the greatest collegiate basketball players.

Both Syracuse and Penn suffered from the loss of men, via the personal foul route. The game was hotly contested from start to finish. Charlie Lee, Syracuse guard, and mainstay in its general defense, was forced from the game on this ruling during the first hold and Harlan Carr went out of the game in the final minutes. Penn lost Captain Davenport and Goldblot via the personal foul route during the latter part of the second half.

At the end of the first half, the Pennsylvania team had a three-point advantage on the Hill team, the score standing at 11 to 8. The Penn team clearly showed during the opening minutes of the game that it was a veteran combination that would give any team in America a real battle. Hanson accounted for the entire eight points that were registered on the Syracuse side of the book in the opening period.

Irving Mendell tallied a field goal for the Orange as the second half started. Mendell, being in the starting lineup for the first time this year, put up a remarkable game.

Hanson tied the score with a foul goal at 11 to 11, and soon afterward put the Syracuse fans into an uproar by tossing in two field baskets to give his team a four-point lead. The Hill team managed to hold the upper hand until the score stood 21 to 17 in their favor with a couple minutes remaining to be played. At this critical time, Monty Chapman, former Syracuse frosh player who was benched as a Penn regular because of absence from the squad the last 10 days, was substituted for Captain Davenport of Penn and made two long field goals to tie the score.

23

Gotch Carr broke the tie with a field goal but this was followed by Scherr's basket and the score was tied at 23 all.

The Penn players were in possession of the ball for the final minutes in the second half and chose to pass the ball around, stalling for the extra five-minute period that would come as a result of the tie score. The visitors evidently feared that if Hanson got the ball, he might dribble through their entire team as he had done on many previous occasions during the evening. Just before the final gun for the second half was sounded, Lindsley tossed the ball, which rimmed the basket and then fell to the floor. The gun had sounded as the ball was in the air.

The first score in the extra period came when Elsemann of Syracuse and Chapman of Penn tossed in goals from the foul line, referee Dowling having called a double foul. With the score tied at 24 to 24, for a couple of minutes the throng in Archbold gymnasium was held spellbound. In the thrilling minutes that followed, Hanson scored two field baskets. Ranage scored a foul goal for Penn between the two Syracuse counters. Just previous to the shot of the gun that ended the combat, Hanson was fouled, and he tossed in two foul goals as the fans surged onto the floor, score Syracuse 30, Penn 25.

24

Skidding the Sport Field With "Skid"

FEBRUARY 25, 1926 | BY LAWRENCE J. SKIDDY, SYRACUSE HERALD

Syracuse University's basketball team last night tumbled from its place at the peak of the collegiate court quintets down to a position alongside Columbia, a team of unquestioned ability, but once defeated. On records, the two share the distinction of being the best the game possesses.

Navy trimmed Columbia, inflicting its lone defeat early in the season. Navy has since been easy for other teams. There was no reason why it should defeat Columbia as it did.

Penn State trimmed Syracuse, stopping a string that had reached 15 consecutive successes. Penn State had been easy for Pittsburgh and other teams. There was no reason why it should score over the Orange, but like Navy in the Columbia game, it did.

The string is broken. Dreams of an undisputed championship fade from the top of Mount Olympus. But the popularity of the team and its members hasn't waned for a moment.

Captain Hanson and his men made a gallant fight in the face of bitter odds to go as far as they did without reverse instead of mourning the fact that defeat finally came. Orange alumni and students would do well to rejoice that it was staved off as long as it was.

Alibis might be unearthed to cover the defeat, but collegiate sport has no place for the alibis. The excuse and the explanation should be left for the professional, the fellow who gets his cash for his performance and

ALL-AMERICAN VIC HANSON

who is expected to come through every time out, regardless. He has no restrictions except to deliver the goods. With the college boy, it is different.

Syracuse might easily have gone on undefeated for the season if Gotch Carr hadn't been declared ineligible. But Carr "cut" classes, and Syracuse is, after all, a university. It is supposed to play basketball and other sports merely as a side entertainment of, by and for its students who are up in their other work. Those down in their work aren't supposed to be even spectators and they certainly cannot compete.

Even with Carr ineligible, Syracuse might have had a champion team without defeat if Bob Lambert, Mike Malster or Irv Mendell had been allowed to play or if Charley Cook had not been hurt. But Lambert, Malster and Mendell all ran afoul of rules, different infractions in each case. And Cook proved that the college boy is only human and subject to injury. All were athletic misfortunes but nevertheless unavoidable as far as the directors of the game would act.

Another alibi might be found in the fact that Lew Andreas, the coach who directed the sensational play of the Orange team for the last three weeks was not available to take charge of last night's game. But the team won other games, games more important in the standpoint of years of rivalry and from teams that were rated as more strong than Penn State with Andreas away early in his illness. So that's that.

The defeat can be accepted without alibi or excuse. It simply came. The team and its followers can rejoice in the fact that throughout the season it has overcome more obstacles in the way of losses of men and coach, played a harder schedule and won a bigger percentage of its games than any team in any sport in the history of the University.

The big and important thing is that Bill Orange is just as good a sport in his disappointment now as the Nittany Lion was during each of the last four years when he dragged his torn and beaten banner off the gridiron.

game summary | february 25, 1926

PENN STATE (37)	fg	ft	t	SYRACUSE (31)	fg	ft	t
Hood, lf	3	2	8	Baker, rf	3	2	8
Roepke, rf	2	3	7	Lee, lg	1	0	2
McDonald, c	2	0	4	Elsemann, c	1	2	4
Vonneids, lg	4	4	12	Richtmeyer, rf	1	3	5
Baron, lg	0	0	0	Tengi, rf	0	0	0
Lunguen, fg	3	0	6	Hanson, lf	6	0	12
Totals	14	9	37	Totals	12	7	31

Score at half time—Penn State, 24, Syracuse, 18.

statistics

Penn Staters Break String Of Orange Five

Nittany Lions Hand Syracuse Basketeers 37 to 31 Reverse

FEBRUARY 25, 1926 | FROM THE SYRACUSE HERALD

State College, Pa.—A grim and determined band of Syracuse University basketball players left here this morning, knowing the taste of defeat for the first time this season, and bound for Rochester where on Friday night they hope to break back into their winning stride again.

Defeat came to the Orange last night by a score of 37 to 31, and it was accomplished in one of the most strange reversals of form ever known to collegiate basketball. Penn State, which has played in mediocre fashion for weeks, arose to championship heights; while Syracuse—always noted for an air tight defense—played rather sloppily on defense all night. Seventeen consecutive victories, two last season and 15 this year, had come since the Orange last tasted defeat.

Penn State caged many of its points on long shots, but nevertheless it worked the ball through the Orange backfield men rather consistently and was the best team of the two for the night at least.

Syracuse showed a splendid offense but, as said before, its defense, usually its strongest point, was weak, and its foul shooting, heretofore one of the brightest features of its play, was far below par. Thus robbed of the two factors that have made it the greatest team in the East, the Orange really had little chance to win.

At the end of the first half, the Nittany Lions were leading 24 to 18. It was the fourth time in 16 games that the Hill team had gone to the locker rooms at half time on the short end of the score; in each of the three previous occasions, the Syracuse team had been able to stage a successful second-half rally.

The Orange made one real bid at the start of the second half, and it did manage to take the lead at 30 to 29, but the effort exhausted the men. Acting Coach McCarthy did not dare use any of his substitutes, and as a result, the tired regulars found themselves forced to surrender.

A brilliant flash by Syracuse marked the closing three minutes. Penn State, leading 35 to 31, decided to "freeze" the ball under its own basket, but on three occasions Lee and Roker got in to take the ball and send it down court. Four times Hanson and Elsemann had shots, and each time they hit the basket, only to roll around and drop outside rather than in. Luck on those four shots spelled the difference between victory and defeat.

THE SYRACUSE NEWSPAPERS

THE SYRACUSE 1925-26 TEAM WAS AGAIN THE HELMS FOUNDATION NATIONAL CHAMPS.
SEATED WITH THE BALL IS STAR VIC HANSON, DIRECTLY IN FRONT OF COACH LEW ANDREAS.

28

ELLIOTT IS BIG STAR IN HILL CLASSIC

CENTER GIVES ORANGE EDGE ALL THE WAY IN TRIUMPH OVER PANTHERS

FEBRUARY 2, 1930 | BY LAWRENCE J. SKIDDY, SYRACUSE HERALD

Syracuse University's high-speed basketeers made a long stride forward in their quest the intercollegiate basketball championship last night when they defeated Pittsburgh by a score of 40 to 29. The Orange triumph was the first defeat of the season for Pittsburgh, which previously had accounted for 12 victories, and more than 3,300 wild, shouting fans were "in on the kill," the number being restricted to less than 4,000 by an athletic office edict that permitted the sale of only 325 general admission tickets.

Absolute domination of the center tap-off by "Slim" Elliott and a remarkable exhibition of play in the following up of shots from both teams by this same athlete gave Syracuse the big edge in the game. Elliott's prowess on the jump and in getting the ball as it careered of the backboard after missed shots gave the Orange possession of the ball three-fourths of the time, and with this ace in the hole the Syracuse sharpshooters capitalized their advantage in fine style.

Ev Katz and Lew Hayman, for Syracuse, and Baker, Pitt's football captain-elect, contributed the scoring thrills of the evening. Katz accounted for 15 of his team's points with seven field goals and a foul, while Hayman was just behind him with six field goals and a foul for 13. Baker contributed 11 points to the Pittsburgh cause on five field goals and a foul.

Hyatt, Pittsburgh's captain and star, who for the last two years led the entire collegiate world in scoring and who is now well in front again with a total of 177 points for 13 games, was held to two field goals and two fouls, a total of six points. Dan Fogarty, accounting for three points himself, attended to Hyatt for 22 minutes, 19 in the first half and three in the second, while George Armstrong handled him for 15 and Warren Stevens for three.

Except for a little nervousness that was in evidence during the first four minutes of play. Syracuse dominated the situation all the way. A foul point started Pitt out in the right direction, and a well-executed center play, one of the few times during the entire night in which Cohen secured the tap, brought W. Kowalis down the court for an easy shot under the basket that he caged in fine fashion. Two minutes later the same athlete broke clear again, and taking a pass from Hyatt, he gave his team a 5-0 advantage.

Here Syracuse took time out, and after returning to the game, the Andreas pupils came through with an exhibition of basketball that was letter perfect. There was no thought in

29

THE SYRACUSE NEWSPAPERS

SYRACUSE'S "REINDEER 5" LED THEIR TEAM TO AN 18-2 RECORD IN 1929-30.
L TO R: CAPTAIN TUPPY HAYMAN, DAN FOGARTY, "SLIM" ELLIOTT,
KEN BEAGLE AND EV KATZ.

their minds that they were playing Pittsburgh, an undefeated team that had won one national championship and was listed as being on its way to another. The Orange simply went out and played basketball.

Elliott did the biggest and the best job of all. He got the tip-offs for them, and he managed to account for the ball four times out of five when it came off the backboards after a missed shot by either team, and with that advantage his mates were ready and willing to do the rest. Fogarty kept Hyatt in leash, and every move was smooth precision.

The Panthers came back strong in the second half and had the ball most of the opening two minutes, but the Orange defense was such that they couldn't penetrate. Pitt was making Hyatt its main threat, and three out of

four of its passes went to him. He couldn't break through. When Armstrong didn't stop him, Hayman, who played the best defensive game of his career, did.

With two members of the second team in play, Syracuse fans began to worry and make inquiry as to time, but their fears were groundless as Syracuse, instead of wilting, spurted in the closing seconds, Katz slipping in one field goal and Stevens corralling another.

Bill McCarthy of New York, as referee, and Howard Ortner, as umpire, turned in one of the finest exhibitions of officiating that Syracuse has seen in a long time. They managed to stay in the background all of the time and let the players have the limelight, but they were sufficiently strict to keep the contest well in hand every minute.

SYRACUSE BASKETBALL: A CENTURY OF MEMORIES

Foul Shots Are Costly to Orange

1946 | BY LAWRENCE J. SKIDDY, SYRACUSE HERALD

New York—Syracuse University's basketball team will be home tonight, having been eliminated by Muhlenberg, 47-41, in last night's first-round game of the National Invitation Basketball Tournament.

The defeat, though merited in many ways, left a bad taste in the mouths of most Orange supporters who saw desperate bids for a second half rally checked by a pair of alert officials, John Nucatola and Louis Eisenstein, who wreaked havoc on Syracuse's ambition by their rulings.

Muhlenberg, a fine basketball team, outplayed Syracuse in the first half, when the Orange tossed away its main opportunity by shooting poorly from the foul line. In the second half, Syracuse made a grand effort and at one time, midway through the half, was only two points in the rear.

At this point, however, it lost its center, Royce Newell, on personal fouls, and from then on it was playing uphill without its greatest asset and with the officials checking most of its bids with rulings it was too rough.

Newell's shoes and the Orange's hectic efforts to close in on a Muhlenberg team that resorted to safety play late in the game did little except to draw foul after foul from the alert referees.

Fifteen of the last 17 fouls called were on Syracuse, and the Orange didn't do well, capitalizing on the few free tries it had.

What fouls meant in this game is best shown by the fact that Syracuse outscored Muhlenberg 18-13 in field goals, but Muhlenberg shot 21 foul points against five for Syracuse.

If ever a game was won and lost from the 15-foot mark, last night's was.

There were 38 fouls called on Syracuse during the night, and Muhlenberg, a remarkably clean team in the eyes of the officiating pair, was guilty of rule infractions that cost free shots just 14 times.

31

Bradley Five Too Fast
for Syracusans

1950 | BY JACK DURKIN, SYRACUSE HERALD

Syracuse players hung up their uniforms today with an 18-9 record for the season after faltering before Bradley in the last 10 minutes of a long campaign.

Ten times in the first half, the score was tied and the lead changed hands several times in a stirring duel. For 30 minutes it was the best battle that had been seen up to that point in any tournament game.

Four big fellows in the Orange array, Ed Miller, Bob Savage, Tom Huggins and Tom Jockle, were combining efforts with Jack Kiley in the early minutes of the second half. Bradley, which had to be satisfied with a 40-39 halftime edge, was thankful for a 60-59 margin after 30 minutes.

Then the combination of Orange "biggies," which had been battling Bradley on even terms was broken, when Miller, the tallest Orange player, fouled out. His height was missed on attack and defense.

After his departure, the Orange could score only twice from the field, and converted three fouls in more than nine waning minutes of play, which amounted to almost the last quarter of the contest.

A combination of able shooting by Gene Melchiorre, who paced the Braves' attack with 20 points, snappy passing, aggressiveness and stamina, marked ball-hawking Bradley's strong finish. The push shot specialists from Peoria piled up 18 points while the faltering Syracusans could produce only seven.

Three other Braves supported Melchiorre with large scoring contributions, in a fast-running, free-shooting attack, with Paul Unruh, Billy Mann and Jim Kelly chipping in with 15, 13 and 11 points, respectively.

Bradley showed it hadn't gone stale following a 10-day layoff since its last victory over Drake. Anderson's boys drew a first-round bye in the tournament, and Syracuse won over Long Island University in its debut.

Four Orange players also hit double figures, Jack Kiley gathering 18, Tom Huggins 16, Tom Jockle 11 and Bob Savage, 10, but Coach Lew Andreas' cagers were outscored both from the field and foul line in their finale.

Kiley brought his total to a new Orange season high of 439 points for 27 contests. Billy Gabor's 409 points in 25 games was the previous high for a Syracuse player in a single season. Had Kiley's team continued in the tournament, he probably would have won the outstanding player award. Jack tallied 39 points in two games, along with acting as a playmaker.

Bradley and Syracuse missed more than their share of fouls, the Braves clicking on 18 of 35 chances, the Orange netting only 14 of 33.

Three Syracuse players were banished via personal fouls: Ed Miller, Dick Suprunowicz and John Beck left the game for the Orange, while Kelly and Elmer Behnke were waved out of the Braves lineup. Suprunowicz had two stitches taken to close a chin cut after the game.

Coach Grady Lewis of the St. Louis Bombers said Savage would be a draft "choice" of his team in the National Basketball Association. Senior Savage, however, may consider playing with the Phillips Oilers of Tulsa, a ranking amateur power, while holding down an engineering position there.

"BULLET" BILLY GABOR WAS A STAR PLAYER FOR SYRACUSE IN THE 1940S. GABOR'S PREVIOUS RECORD OF 409 POINTS FOR A SYRACUSE PLAYER IN A SINGLE SEASON WAS BROKEN BY JACK KILEY.

THE SYRACUSE NEWSPAPERS

Wedding Bells Break Up Orange Lineup

Huggins Lost for Tournament

MARCH 30, 1951 | FROM THE POST-STANDARD

Peoria, Ill.—Dan Cupid may cut down Syracuse University's basketball cagers here tonight in the semifinal round of the National Campus Basketball Tourney, where the favored Toledo Rockets failed Wednesday when Coach Marc Guley's deep squad ran off with a 69-52 conquest.

The cutie with the bow and arrow took aim and landed a bulls-eye at Bill Orange's ace rebounder, Tom Huggins, some time ago, so Tall Tom won't be with the New Yorkers when they face the rugged Utah Utes in tonight's second game of a twin bill. Bradley faces Wyoming in the other contest. The finals will be held Saturday.

Huggins, a junior, who played sensationally off the boards, in Syracuse's surprising triumph over the Rockets-tossing in a dozen big points to boot-made plans months ago to get married March 31, long after everyone figured the basketball season would be completed. Plans already made, invitations printed and mailed, plus a host of other commitments forced the likable GI to leave by plane yesterday so that he could make tomorrow's noon wedding in Port Dickinson (just outside of Binghamton).

Guley, therefore, faces a rebounding problem in tonight's opening battle against a Utah team that also surprised when they eliminated the favored contingent from Villanova, 67-65. The chances are that Guley will shift the veteran Tony Hladik into Huggins' spot, with Chuck Steveskey and Frank Reddout also on deck.

The victory over Toledo was a true team effort with the point-scoring being spread among 11 members. Big Ed Miller contributed 18 big points, but Jack Kiley and Tom Jockle, both with seven each, set up a number of clever scoring plays, as the Orangemen's ball-handling and savvy made the biggest impression of any of the fives in opening-round play.

Utah, coached by the veteran Vadal Peterson, has a 22-12 record. They have three wins to their credit this year over Brigham Young, NIT champion, and have licked Denver, Stanford, St. Joseph's, Wyoming, Oregon and others. They lost by only one point to St. John's in New York's Garden during the regular season.

They have an outstanding playmaker in Jim Cleverly (5-9), and a great scorer in Glen Smith (6-4), a hook-shot artist. The rest of the starting five is composed of Glen Duggins (6-1), Ken Bates (6-5), and Paul Shrum (6-2), defensive ace, who will try to stop Kiley.

Syracuse Wins 76-75; Had Been 20 Points Bad

Victory One of Most Amazing Games of Year

APRIL 1, 1951 | FROM THE POST-STANDARD

Peoria, Ill.—Staging the most amazing comeback of the collegiate basketball season, Syracuse University's basketball team rallied from a 20-point, first-quarter deficit to edge Bradley's Braves, 76 to 75, in a hectic finale to the National Campus Basketball Tournament in the Bradley fieldhouse before a vociferous crowd of about 8,600 fans.

Much the underdog and having been defeated previously by Bradley in the Sugar Bowl tournament, Coach Mare Guley's Orangemen staged a furious rally in the final three minutes after Big Ed Miller, a tower of strength off the boards, had been ousted on personal fouls.

The Orange cagers trailed by a point, 66-65, at this point, but Jack Kiley arched in a long set, and Stan Swanson stole the ball to drive thru for a layup. He added a foul point on the play.

Gene Melchiorre hit on a follow shot, but Frank Reddout, another stellar sub, rang up a three-pointer, and Swanson drove through for another hoop for a 75-68 edge. Swanson also added another foul for the final Orange point.

Bradley, aided by traveling calls by the officials, notched baskets by Buzz Ott, Melchiorre, Fred Schlictman and a foul by Preece to complete its scoring.

Preece's foul point called for an extra Syracuse time out, and Bradley, trailing by only a point, missed its chance for a winning basket in the last eight seconds, getting possession after the technical.

The host Braves from Peoria opened up on all cylinders at the opening tip-off as they rolled in five points during the first 48 seconds on Melchiorre's gift shot and two nifty baskets by Schlictman.

After Behnke's rebound shot made it 7-0, Guley took his starting Orange lineup out and inserted the second team of Bob Roche, Bill Manikas, Stan Swanson, Charley Stevesky and Frank Reddout.

Behnke followed with a free throw, however, and a gift shot by Grover, Melchiorre's pivot shot, rebounds by Behnke and Schlictman and a fast-break bucket by Grover gave the red-hot Braves an 18-0 lead after 3:46 of playing time had elapsed.

Roche finally drove in under the basket and ended the cold streak for the Orange with 5:49 to go in the first period.

Melchiorre and Schlictman hit two quick baskets for Bradley to make it 22-2, but Roche hit from the free throw line, and the Orange started to climb back.

Manikas hit a set shot and, after a pivot shot by Melchiorre, Ed Miller reentered the lineup, and the Orange starters began to come back in.

Steveskey hit a free throw and Suprunowicz drove in full speed for a layup to slash the lead to 24-8.

Miller hit from the pivot, and Steveskey followed with a hook shot to make it 24-12.

Schlictman interrupted the Orange comeback with a free throw, but another Steveskey hook and a pair of free throws by Swanson cut Bradley's lead to 25-16 at the quarter.

The hot-scoring pace subsided for the first minute and a half of the second period, but Grover's jumpshot stopped the deep freeze and Suprunowicz connected on the fast break to leave the score 27-18, Bradley.

Jack Kiley reentered the lineup, and after Kelly hit from the free throw line, the Orange captain hit a set shot to reduce the host's lead to 28-20.

Schlictman's jump shot stretched the Brave lead back to 30-20, and Melchiorre's two gift shots matched Kiley's under-the-basket effort and left the margin at 10 points.

With 4:45 of the half left, the score was 34-24, in Bradley's favor, after Suprunowicz and Melchiorre had matched baskets.

Suprunowicz, playing terrific ball, drove in for another two points. Jockle hit off the pivot, and Suprunowicz took a hand-off and scored to put Syracuse right back into the game as they trailed, 34-30.

Kelly's gift shot stretched the lead to 35-30, but Jockle hit a free throw and Kiley drove around Grover and scored to make it 35-33. and Syracuse, trailing by but two points, had made an amazing recovery.

Behnke's rebound stretched the lead back to four points and, after Jockle and Melchiorre matched gift shots, Melchiorre hit a 20-foot set shot to give the Braves a 40-34 lead.

Kiley's gift shot at the half left the Orange trailing, 40-35.

Finally, after three minutes of scoreless play in the second half, Jockle hit a 20-foot one-hander, and 30 seconds later, Kiley added a fast-break hook to bring the Orange to within one point of Bradley at 40-39.

At this point it was the Braves, not Syracuse who were cold, and a brilliant drive in by Suprunowicz put the Orange in front for the first time, 41-40, with 6:14 of the third period left.

Miller's pair of gifts shots on Behnke's fourth foul put Syracuse ahead, 43-40.

Schlictman scored Bradley's first points of the second half with a jump shot with 3:10 of the period left, but Kiley countered with a 30-footer to leave Syracuse ahead, 45-42.

Free throws by Kelly and Melchiorre reduced Syracuse's lead to one point. The lead diminished when Mann's rebound put the Braves back in front, 46-45.

Bradley stretched its streak to nine consecutive points on a pair of gift shots and a pivot shot by Grover and Schlictman's free throw to make the score Bradley 51, Syracuse 45.

Roche's gift shot and two more from the bread line by Miller brought the Orange back to within three points at 51-48, but Bradley countered with free tosses by Grover and Schlictman to lead by five.

Preece scored on a fast break to lift the host's lead to 55-48, but Miller's gift shot and a rebound by Jockle made it Bradley 55, Syracuse 51 at the three-quarter post.

Swanson's 13-footer after 30 seconds of the final frame had slashed Bradley's lead to two points, and Kiley sank a pair of free throws to knot the count at 55-55.

Schlictman's 30-foot kiss broke the tie, and after another charity throw by Miller,

JACK KILEY AVERAGED 15.1 PPG DURING HIS THREE-YEAR VARSITY CAREER, ENDING IN 1951. KILEY WAS THE ONLY ORANGEMAN TO SCORE MORE THAN 400 POINTS IN EACH OF TWO SEASONS UNTIL VINNIE COHEN IN 1957.

Swanson's tip-in reduced the deficit to three points and after Kelly made a free throw, a rebound by Kiley and Swanson's jump shot tied the count at 64-64.

Behnke's rebound put Bradley back in front, but Manikas scored a gift shot to reduce the lead to one point.

Miller left the game with five personals with 3:42 to go, but Behnke missed the free throw and Kiley engineered a 25-foot set with 3:26 to go to put Syracuse in front, 67-66.

Swanson's steal and subsequent basket and free throw put the Orange ahead, 70-66.

Melchiorre's rebound cut the Orange lead to two points, but Reddout's basket and free throw and a pivot shot and gift shot by Swanson gave the Orange a 70-68 with 1:54 of play left.

Bradley rallied furiously, however, and Macuga's left-hander, Melchiorre's hook shot and Schlictman's jump shot reduced the lead to 76-74 as the Orange attempted to stall.

Kelly's pivot bucket put Syracuse behind, 59-56.

A layup by Buzz Ott and Grover's pivot shot put Bradley in front, 63-56, with 6:25 to play, and Syracuse called time out.

With 5:53 to play, Mann fouled out for Bradley, and Miller sank both free shots to make the score Bradley 63, Syracuse 58.

The Orange stayed in the game as

With eight seconds left, Syracuse had the ball but called time out number six which made a technical foul. Aaron Preece hit the free throw to cut the lead to one point, and the Braves received possession of the ball.

They were unable to score during the last eight futile seconds.

37

Orange Ends with Win Over Rhode Island

MARCH 3, 1956 | BY BILL REDDY, THE POST-STANDARD

Syracuse and LeMoyne finished their seasons with victories last night, the Orange trouncing Rhode Island, 106-82, and the Dolphins routing Siena, 82-59.

The smallest turnout of the doubleheader season, 1,621, made enough noise to split eardrums, as many of the fans brought musical instruments, including drums, and the bedlam never stopped in the second game. It was LeMoyne's 16th win against seven losses, while Siena now has won seven, lost 13.

The Syracuse total equalled the all-time high for an Orange cage team. The previous high of 106 was set against Oswego State in 1945.

Both the Rams and the Orange showed some hot shooting in the closely fought first half, but early in the second half, Syracuse turned on an unstoppable fast-break attack that left the visitors trailing wearily.

Vince Cohen maintained his place as the top scorer for the Orange campaign as he popped in 29 points in the finale.

Ron Marozzi, who got 19 points in the first half, tired badly in the second half, but finished with 24 points to lead the visitors, who suffered their 13th loss in 24 games. For Syracuse, it was the 14th win against eight losses.

The consistently hot marksmanship of Coach Marc Guley's team is shown in the statistics, which credited the winners with 45 field goals in 79 shots, an average of better than 55 percent. Meanwhile, Rhode Island was hitting 30 for 83.

Cohen sank 13 fielders in 18 attempts, while Ron Gillespie had 10 assists.

Jim Snyder, with 18, Jim Brown with 17, Gary Clark with 14 and Gillespie, also with 14, were other double-figure scorers for Syracuse.

BOB JOHNSTON, THE SYRACUSE NEWSPAPERS

SU's 1956-57 TEAM
WAS THE SCHOOL'S
FIRST EVER IN AN
NCAA TOURNAMENT.

game summary | march 3, 1956

SYRACUSE (106)	g	f-t	t	RHODE ISLAND (82)	g	f-t	t
Cohen	13	3-3	29	Von Weyhe	7	4-6	18
Aloise	1	0-0	2	Schult	0	0-0	0
Clark	6	2-4	14	Anderson	4	0-0	8
Brown	8	7-10	17	Haworth	1	1-3	3
Evans	2	0-0	4	Stairs	4	0-1	8
Snyder	8	2-4	18	Adams	1	1-2	3
Crofoot	0	0-0	0	Kohlstat	0	0-0	0
Gilespie	6	2-4	14	Madreperia	5	3-4	15
Holnbeck	1	0-0	2	Sothworth	0	3-4	3
Loudis	2	0-1	4	Marozzi	8	10-12	24
Albanese	1	0-0	2				
Stark	0	0-0	0				
Totals	45	16-26	106	Totals	30	22-32	82

| statistics

39

SU Rallies to Win NCAA Opener

Fast-Break Attack Cuts Down UCONN

MARCH 13, 1957 | BY BILL REDDY, THE POST-STANDARD

New York—Trailing by 10 points with eight minutes to play, Syracuse University's basketeers turned on a dazzling fast-break attack that swept them past University of Connecticut for a dramatic 82-76 victory in the opener of a Madison Square Garden triple header tonight.

With Vinnie Albanese setting up the plays and with Gary Clark out-racing defenders for easy layups, the Orangemen turned a tight contest into an impressive victory.

Clark finished as high man in the game with 26 points, despite a long rest after he had been charged with his fourth personal foul. Vinnie Cohen, Brooklyn ace whose marksmanship kept the Hillmen in threatening position most of the way, was close behind with 23.

The victory over the UConns, who had suffered a one-point loss to the Orangemen in January on the Connecticut court, marked the opening of first-round play in the Eastern Regional National Collegiate Athletic Association tournament.

By winning, coach Marc Guley's team qualified for second-round play, and will face Lafayette, Middle Atlantic Conference champions, in the Philadelphia Palestra Friday night. Doubleheaders will be played in Philadelphia Friday and Saturday, with the winner qualifying for the national semifinals at Kansas City the following weekend.

Outrebounded by the aggressive UConns most of the way, forced to gamble for long shots against the rugged, sliding-zone defense of coach Hugh Greer's team, the Orangemen trailed through most of the first half, and faltered badly when Clark went out, carrying four personals, with 14 minutes left to play.

When the sharpshooting and confident UConns made it 65-55, with eight minutes left, Syracuse called time out and went into an all-court press. The move seemed to upset the timing of the UConns and helped to set up a couple of quick, easy layups by Cohen and Clark.

Then, while the Huskies suddenly seemed to lose their shooting ability and their poise, the galloping Orangemen swept through an incredible sequence. They scored 22 points while Connecticut was getting just three, and within the space of six minutes, Syracuse was transformed from a well-beaten team to a romping-home victor.

Cohen, Clark, Snyder, Cincebox and Breland all clicked in this Albanese drive, as Guley gambled with all the height he could muster. Within three minutes, Syracuse had gone out in front of Connecticut on a push shot by Snyder, 69-68, and when Cincebox sank a layup on a three-point attempt, Clark rebounded on the missed free throw.

On top by 71-68, Syracuse froze the ball for about 25 seconds, bidding to draw the UConns out of their zone, and it worked well enough to set up Cincebox for another layup.

Syracuse's 1957 starting five were the first Syracuse team in the NCAAs. From left, Manny Breland, Gary Clark, Jon Cincebox, Jim Snyder and Vinnie Cohen.

Breland stole the ball for a fast-break layup. Snyder intercepted a pass to set up a pair of free throws by Breland, and, with 2:10 left, Syracuse was out in front by 77-68.

Connecticut's fine battlers struck back, with Jim O'Connor sinking a layup and Al Cooper stealing a pass-in for another layup.

Syracuse took time out then, and Connecticut used a pressing defense all the way to the end-line. This was duck soup for the eager Orangemen, who on two occasions just lobbed the ball downcourt, confident that Clark could outrace anyone on the Connecticut team. He did, too, for unopposed layups.

O'Connor, a fine 6-1 push-shot specialist, led the losers with 21 points, while Al Cooper,

6-7 1/2, and Bill Schmidt, 6-6, not only added 19 and 14 points, respectively, but also grabbed 16 rebounds apiece.

Clark, who along with Cincebox and Snyder was blocked out strongly in the early play, led Syracuse with 11 rebounds, a figure matched by Bob Osborne of Connecticut. Strangely, when the game was over, official statistics showed each team with 51 rebounds, but that hardly seemed credible, for Connecticut appeared to have too long a lead in that department for Syracuse ever to catch up.

Syracuse got four more field goals, sinking 33 of 79 attempts while the UConns made good on 29 of 73 from the floor. Syracuse missed nine of 25 free throws compared with six of 24 missed by the losers.

41

SYRACUSE BOWS OUT OF NCAA WITH 67-58 LOSS

MARCH 17, 1957 | BY ARNIE BURDICK, SYRACUSE HERALD

Philadelphia—North Carolina's imported basketball team had too much poise, height and shooting ability for Syracuse here in the Palestra last night.

As a result of their 67-58 triumph, the Tar Heels captured the Eastern Regional NCAA crown, and thus qualified for next week's National Collegiate Championship finals at Kansas City.

The Orange, cold from the field and cooler from the charity stripe, could not match the smoother ball-handling of the "New York Southerners," paced by All-American Lennie Rosenbluth and Tommy Kearns.

This pair did the major damage, though countless calls by officials Jack MacPherson and Joe Conway puzzled the 6,431 rooters.

The Orange opened strongly, with sophomore Jon Cincebox replacing the injured Vinnie Albanese in the starting cast. Cincebox, a 6-7 rebounder, helped the Orange around the boards as Syracuse stayed even with the nation's No. 1 team for seven minutes.

It was 12-all at this juncture, when Cincebox was charged with his third personal foul. Albanese replaced him, and the Orange immediately went into an all-court press.

As Syracuse missed 11 straight free throws, Carolina ran nine straight points to draw away to a 21-12 spread.

From this splurge, Syracuse never recovered, though Albanese and Vinnie Cohen, the game's top scorer with 25 points, popped in two from the field to close the gap.

The Tar Heel leaders; Rosenbluth, who hit 23, Brennan, 23, and Kearns, 22, recovered their touch and opened up a 37-28 halftime edge.

Gary Clark, held to 11 points, opened play after intermission on a fast-break goal to cut the margin to seven. The Orange never drew any closer, as the poised Rebels controlled the ball and quickly opened up a 54-38 advantage, as Kearns' driving and dribbling broke the game open.

Syracuse did manage to score seven more field goals than the (24-17), but the Orange got licked at the free-throw line, 33-10.

Syracuse made only 10 of its 23 from the foul line, though eight or nine more should be charged against the Orange for failing to hit on the first of their "one-and-one" opportunities. Carolina had 45 free-throw attempts.

JIM SNYDER (50) OF SYRACUSE AND DANNY LOTZ (33) OF NORTH CAROLINA MOMENTARILY LOSE SIGHT OF THE BALL AS THE TWO GO AFTER A REBOUND IN THE 1957 NCAA EASTERN REGIONAL FINAL.

ORANGE CAGERS END LOSS STRING

MURRAY GETS WINNING GOAL AGAINST BC

MARCH 4, 1962 | FROM THE POST-STANDARD

Boston—Syracuse terminated its 27-game losing streak when Bob Murray's twisting layup dropped through the string with only 11 seconds to play to give the Orangemen a 73-to-72 victory over Boston College here Saturday afternoon.

Boston College was off and running at the outset, jumping to a 24-17 lead at the half-way mark of the first period.

But Syracuse, spurred by sophomore guard Carl Vernick, whose faultless driving kept the BC defenders running all afternoon, held BC scoreless for six straight minutes and outscored the Eagles, 16 to 2, over a seven-minute stretch to take a 33-26 lead.

Leading 41-35 at the half, Syracuse got in foul trouble at the start of the second half as BC converted eight straight free throws while only Herb Foster countered with a basket for Syracuse as BC trailed only 43-32. Billy Donovan of Boston College started to hit with his two-handed jump shot and BC started to come back.

With Donovan and Jim Hooley, who both scored 20 points, scoring well, BC tied the score at 60-60 with slightly more than four minutes to play and Syracuse called time out.

The Orangemen, who had lost 22 straight games this season, spurted for seven straight points as Vernick converted on a three-point play and sophomore Jim Seaman tallied on a three-on-one situation.

Three BC baskets made it 67-66 before Murray hit a jumper and made a free throw to make it 70-66.

Trailing 71-63, BC went on to hit 72-71 as Hooley swished a jumper and made a pair of free throws. It was BC's first lead since the nine-minute mark of the first half.

Then Murray, who scored 11 of his 17 points in the second half, twisted down the base line and sidearmed his layup through the strings for the winner.

BASKETBALL COACH MARC GULEY WITH PLAYERS ERNIE DAVIS (24), JOHN MACKEY (35) AND DON KING, ALL OF WHOM ALSO PLAYED FOR THE FOOTBALL TEAM.

Duke's Surge Spoils Syracuse Bid

Bing Has Cold Night

MARCH 13, 1966 | BY ARNIE BURDICK, THE POST-STANDARD

Raleigh, N.C.—Massive, hot-shooting Duke had to beat back several spectacular Syracuse rallies before capturing the NCAA Eastern Regional Championship here last evening, 91-81.

A pro-Duke sellout throng of 12,400 fans roared their approval as their heroes won their way into the semifinals of the national championship to be played next weekend on the University of Maryland campus.

It was a thrilling battle, with the Orange overcoming a poor start and the coldest night of the winter for their All-America hero Dave Bing.

Down midway in the first half by 16 big points—31-15—the Orange continued to saw wood behind the aggressive efforts of George Hicker and Vaughn Harper. After they closed the gap to only 44-37 at the half, Syracuse finally shot into the lead midway in the second half on a brilliant three-point play by Harper 58-55.

The Orange continued to keep the heat on the Devils and made it 62-58 shortly thereafter. But by this time, both Bing and Harper had four fouls on them and had to play carefully. Little Richie Cornwall and Jim Boeheim, a pair of pepperpots, tied the heated encounter at 64, 66 and 68-all, and Hicker's long jumper made it 70-all with 6:35 left.

Two hoops by Boeheim put the Orange in front again 74-72, before Duke went on the first of two six-point sprees to lock up the

DAVE BING IS CONSIDERED BY MANY TO BE THE GREATEST OF ALL SYRACUSE PLAYERS. HE PLAYED FROM 1963 TO 1966.

THE SYRACUSE NEWSPAPERS

game. It was during the first of these two Duke bursts that the Orange lost Harper on fouls, and they were never again able to battle the Dukes under the boards.

Leading the Duke avalanche were All-America Jack Marin, with 22, and their two backcourt wizards, Bob Verga, with 21, and Steve Vacendak, with 19. Tops for the Orange was Hicker with 17, followed by Rick Dean with 16, Boeheim with 15 and Harper with 13. Bing was held to only 10 points, 20 under his season-long pace.

The tall Devils tossed up a rugged 3-2 zone against the Orange, and this kept Syracuse firing away from well outside. Bing, especially, couldn't hit—he was 4 for 14 from the field for the night—and the Orange weren't able to get many rebounds off their offensive board, either, during the early going.

When they finally came to life, they were getting easier shots from close in. But down the stretch, when it counted, Syracuse seemed to be content to try its luck from well out.

Vacendak, a rugged boy from Scranton, Pennsylvania, did most of the work in tying up Dave, but the sliding zone of Duke gave him plenty of help.

THE SYRACUSE NEWSPAPERS

Vaughn Harper demonstrates the rebounding ability that earned him the title "Kangaroo Kid."

Overall, Syracuse made only 31 of 75 from the floor to Duke's blazing 31 of 60. The Devils also had more free-throw chances as Syracuse had to foul their taller opponents. Duke was 29 of 37 from the line, while Syracuse was nearly perfect—19 of 21—but didn't get enough opportunities.

46

JIM BOEHEIM AS A PLAYER.

47

'MURPH' MANGLES
MANLEY MARKS

1967 | BY BOB SNYDER, SYRACUSE HERALD-JOURNAL

Jim Maloney is a talkative young coach when his team wins.

His team is Calvin Murphy, and a supporting cast. Last night, before a preseason "sell-out" crowd of some 2,200 empty seats, Niagara's sophomore sensation did what comes naturally, and the bit players also gave five-star performances in whipping Syracuse, 116-107 at Manley Field House.

Maloney told us, after his 5-9 $\frac{1}{2}$ whiz poured in a record 50 points (Dave Bing had 43 here against Buffalo in the 1965-66 season), that "Calvin is unhappy at Niagara. I know he is looking around (at other campuses). He can't win with this frosh club, and he doesn't want to play with a loser."

True, that frosh quintet is a loser. Al Butler's yearlings were crushed by the Tangerines, 116-63, in the prelim of a twin bill that drew only 4,072 fans and thousands more watching via the boob tube. My, how those sellouts are costing SU money.

Roy Danforth played his subs much of the way in a game that never was: The Hill frosh, winners of 24 straight, shot an incredible 76.1 percent (54 of 71) as North Syracusan John Unger led the way with 27 points.

Calvin, now averaging 39.5 and second to LSU stringbean Pete Maravich, wouldn't comment on rumors that he might transfer to Houston in the fall. When asked, The Marvelous One replied, "My coach told me not to answer that question."

But Maloney fielded it, adding, "the pressure has been relieved since I announced my resignation. We've won three of five and were in the other two (Niagara is 8-8 this season)." Maloney may be a lame duck coach, but apparently he's still the boss with his players.

The "Little Fella," so-called by Maloney, also set three other Manley marks: points in a half, 34; free throws made (20) and attempted (23) in a game. His 28 shots (he connected on 15) tied yet another court record, although it's below his average tries this winter (32).

"I was able to shoot in the first half (against SU's man-to-man)," Murphy said, "but with the box-and-one in the last half, I passed off more and took him (Rich Cornwall) inside, leaving Mike Brown (and others) free.

"Did you see my teammates?" the muscular Murphy added. "See 'em pick 'n roll? They made it easy to score 50 and only shoot 28 times."

Easy? Who works one-on-one as much as Calvin Murphy?

But Murphy's supporting cast did play well. Manny Leaks (6-8), who always seems to come up with a big game against SU, dominated the Eagles' board in the first half. And that took away a portion of Fred Lewis' game plan—to break John Suder, or whomever was on Murphy, downcourt after Calvin shot for a possible "cherry" (easy layup).

That went down the drain and so did playing Calvin man-to-man without any help. In the first half, Murphy scored 34 as Lewis shuttled Suder, Bob Clary and Ray Balukas in an out.

Murphy either faked them out and tossed in 15-20 footers, or spent time at the free-throw line as the Orange dropped No. 4 in a row.

But after SU (now 6-9) fell behind, 67-49 at halftime, the Orange switched to the box-and-one. And not only did Cornwall do a good job at the head of the defense, but the cornermen began to pick up Murphy in deep, something they failed to do in the first 20 minutes.

Also, the SU press midway in the last half looked like the Orange press of old—forcing opponents into turnovers and setting up Hill buckets, as well. "I'd have to say this was as good as we can play," Lewis said. "The press finally got going, Wayne Ward made moves we'd been waiting to see all season, and Richie played a fine all-around game (10 of 14) from the head of the key."

One of the major faults of the SU offense in the second half was the failure to penetrate inside in an attempt to foul out Leaks, who committed his fourth personal just 2:06 into the half. And Murphy, who picked up No. 4 with 11:42 remaining, also finished the game.

Although guilty of a few errant passes on fast breaks, a problem all season for SU, Vaughn Harper had his best offensive night (32 points) and teamed well with Ward off the boards.

Perhaps the unsung hero for the Purple Eagles, as he's been other times this winter, was Murphy's running mate, Brown. He converted three steals into baskets within five minutes when SU was rallying (never within seven) in the second half, and was 8 of 9 on fielders.

49

THE SYRACUSE NEWSPAPERS

(LEFT) GREG "KID" KOHLS, ONE OF SYRACUSE'S GREATEST LONG-RANGE SHOOTERS, PLAYED BEFORE THE THREE-POINT SHOT. (BELOW) DENNIS DUVAL (22) LOOKS TO PASS.

THE SYRACUSE NEWSPAPERS

SYRACUSE BASKETBALL: A CENTURY OF MEMORIES

AW SHOOT, RUTGERS PINS ORANGE BY 1

FEBRUARY 7, 1975 | BY BOB SNYDER, SYRACUSE HERALD-JOURNAL

It must have been ol' Doc Naismith who first said it, when he invented the game of basketball.

If you don't shoot, you can't score. And if you don't score, you can't win.

Without meaning to, Syracuse tried to beat Rutgers by not shooting in the second half. It didn't work. So when last night's vocal Manley Field House crowd of 7,125 heard the postgame announcement that co-captain Jimmy Lee was selected as the recipient of the annual Varsity Club Night trophy as SU's most valuable player in the game, no one cared. Not even Jimmy Lee.

Moments earlier, he'd hit the Manley tartan as a two-man halfcourt trap produced no whistle. But it did bring to a stunning end SU's 15-game winning steak under the Manley Dome. Mike Dabney came away with the ball, drove to the hoop, and was fouled in the act of shooting by Lee's backcourt mate, Jimmy Williams (despite Bug's bid to draw an offensive foul). With 42 seconds remaining, Dabney canned two free throws, giving Tom Young's 19th-ranked Scarlet Knights (16-4) a well-deserved 76-75 win over SU.

Roy Danforth's Orangemen (13-5), who'd won 51 of their last 52 at Manley and last lost at home to Connecticut (61-60 a year ago), had two more possessions. But not a shot was fired by the favored host quintet in those agonizing final 42 ticks of the clock.

Rudy Hackett (19 points, 16 rebounds) threw the ball away. But SU regained possession on a travel violation. Then, in a last bid for the game-winner, a pass into Hackett (who managed just four second-half shots) was deflected. Rutgers took over. Dabney was fouled with two seconds left, missed the free throw, but the horn sounded before frosh Marty Byrnes could try flipping in Hackett's long pass.

In fact, SU could not even initiate a shot-a-minute offense in the second half. "You can't beat anybody," Danforth said, "shooting 19 shots in a half . . . . We had no movement on offense. We lost all of it. We got out of our offense . . . . We seem to get more movement with Rudy at forward, rather than center.

"But that's my fault. I had the offense in front of me. I called the plays the second half . . . . I guess we tried to go to Hackett too much. Rutgers was doing a good job sloughing back in on him. We probably should have run more perimeter stuff. We talked about it at halftime, but we just didn't do it."

The fact remains in almost every game this season, SU has gone down the stretch with Hackett at center.

"This was one of our most difficult wins," said Young, whose Knights have beaten SU twice in a row, but trail in the series, 13-8. With a young (no seniors played), but experienced club, Young was pleased that "we didn't try and make up those 10 points (that SU led by at half-time) in 30 seconds. We were patient."

What Rutgers did was play more team basketball after intermission. All-American candidate Phil Sellers (20 points, 12 rebounds, three straight assists at the start of the second half) explained it this way:

MIKE LEE (25) DRIBBLES THE BALL AGAINST FURMAN.

"We weren't gonna win with long jumpers." So when the 6-5 junior wasn't shooting (he was 7-for-14), he was assisting or rebounding—despite SU's bid to contain him. Sellers put on a superb second-half show.

'snyde' remarks | f e b r u a r y 7, 1 9 7 5

| by bob snyder |

SU center Earnie Seibert was sidelined the entire second half because, Danforth said, "The doctor told us he was fatigued, dehydrated, couldn't play anymore (although he went just the first 12:16 of the game)." Seibert did not play at all in Tuesday's win at St. Bonaventure because of a virus . . . . SU went from even to down five during the ten minutes Williams sat down in the middle of last half. He penetrates better than any SU guard . . . . Sease also sat for eight minutes during that stretch . . . . Two technicals against sub center Bob Parker for grabbing the rim proved very costly.

SU shot 52.7 percent (29 of 55), and was 10 of 19 in the second half. Rutgers hit on 49.3 percent (33 of 67), but blistered cords last half (62.1 percent, 18 of 29) . . . . Lee was 8 of 16, Hackett 7 of 11 (far too few shots), Sease 3 of 9, Williams 5 of 10. Starters scored all Rutgers' points. Sellers was 8 of 14, frosh Hollis Copeland 8 of 16 (while scoring 12 of his 18 the last half), Dabney 7 of 14, Jordan 7 of 13 . . . . SU had 17 of its 28 turnovers after intermission, Rutgers 23.

52

MOUNTAINEERS CHILL
ORANGE, 84-81

WVU TRAILED BY 21

FEBRUARY 9, 1975 | BY BOB SNYDER, SYRACUSE HERALD AMERICAN

Syracuse University's basketball team was on the brink of cracking the Top Twenty just a few days ago. But that was before SU devised new and interesting ways to blow a game at home in the second half, yesterday afternoon's collapse producing an 84-81 upset victory for West Virginia.

Roy Danforth's Orangemen (13-6), on top by 21 on two occasions in the first half and ahead at halftime, 52-33, produced a first. This marked the first time since Danforth inherited a losing 1968-69 club (his first as head coach) that SU has dropped two straight at Manley Field House. The Orange saw a 10-point intermission advantage over Rutgers go down the drain (76-75) here Thursday. Prior to that, SU seemed close to invincible under the Manley Dome, where they'd won 15 in a row, 51 out of 52.

That Manley mystique has been shattered. And with it went hopes for any national recognition. To make matters worse, 11-point favorite SU had the added exposure of being on the ECAC's televised game of the week yesterday. But those boob tube viewers who didn't turn off the set at halftime and the 5,329 fans under the Manley Dome witnessed a classic second-half display by SU of how not to play basketball.

In winning for the first time at Manley, first-year head coach Joedy Gardner's Mountaineers (12-7) deserve plenty of credit for not packing it in, rallying from such a deficit on the road. WVU won it in the final 15 seconds from the foul line, where their accuracy was only 40 percent until freshman Maurice Robinson made both ends of a one-and-one free throw situation. A scholastic All-American, the 6-7 Robinson was shooting a horrendous 30 percent (9-for-30) at the charity stripe before yesterday—and those were his lone attempts of the game. They gave WVU an 82-81 lead.

SU's final bid to win it was a poor example of shot selection. Kevin King tossed up a foul-line turnaround jumper that wouldn't have connected, but SU's top gun, Rudy Hackett (26 points, 14 rebounds), was called for offensive goaltending with six seconds remaining. Two seconds later, Hackett committed his fifth foul, and the Mountaineers' best player, 6-7 junior Warren Baker, canned two free throws in a one-and-one opportunity, making it 84-81.

53

There was nothing for Syracuse to do but play it out and head for a dressing room chewing out from Danforth. The Orangemen had snatched defeat from the jaws of victory.

"If we keep playing this way," Danforth told his squad, "we're gonna lose 3-4 more games, get beaten out in the ECAC tournament (qualifier for the NCAAs) and watch the NIT (National Invitation Tournament) on television. We're too good a club for that to happen . . . Nobody on this club can win games by themselves. But some guys have been trying to lately. You win as a team and lose as a team. And in these last two, I don't like the way we're losing."

SU registered only 10 second-half field goals in just 29 attempts (10 more than the no-shoot exhibition against Rutgers). SU wound up shooting 45.3 percent (34-for-75), WVU 51.4 percent (38-for-74).

"I don't believe you have to get the boards," said Gardner. "I'm a believer in the high-percentage shot . . . Our only important halftime adjustment was going with the man to man."

It was SU being aggressive under the boards, while WVU showed no desire to block out on its defensive board, which played a key in the Orange first-half domination.

"We forgot how we got ahead," Danforth said. "We just stand around and watch the game. Those five (SU players on the court) ought to have bought tickets. They had the best seats in the house . . . . They (WVU) won it from the foul line. They just wanted it more than we did. We must be getting complacent.

"A kick in the rear might do some good . . . . The Intramural All-Stars played better than we did."

JIMMY LEE (10) AND RUDY HACKETT.

54

HACKETT NETS 30 FOR SU

MARCH 16, 1975 | BY BOB SNYDER, SYRACUSE HERALD AMERICAN

Philadelphia—Rudy Hackett said he'd never forget those two missed free throws with 17 seconds remaining in regulation in last year's NCAA overtime loss to Oral Roberts.

He and his Syracuse University teammates proved it last night, when the Orangemen made their last 13 straight pressure free throws en route to a thrilling 87-83 overtime victory over LaSalle in the nightcap of an NCAA East Regional twin bill before a jammed house of 9,233 screaming fans in the Palestra. Kansas State upset Penn 69-62 in the opener.

Hackett led SU (21-7) with 30 points, fellow co-captain Jimmy Lee scoring 20, and Nottingham product Chris Sease scoring 18 before fouling out with the score tied and 1:57 remaining in regulation. Joe Bryant (25), who fouled out with SU ahead by two and 1:42 left in overtime, and Bill Taylor (20) paced the Explorers (22-7), the East Coast Conference champions. Guards Glen Collier and Charlie Wise added 16 and 14, respectively.

SU never trailed in overtime. Hackett, who was 11-for-19 from the field, 8 of 10 at the foul line, made both ends of a one-and-one free-throw opportunity nine seconds into OT, breaking the regulation deadlock of 71-all. Wise's steal and two free throws tied it with 4:23 to go. Then, reserve Kevin King (who did a solid 25-minute job at forward and guard) hit from the top of the key at the 4:06 mark. And when Hackett grabbed an offensive rebound (one of his 12 caroms), he was fouled on the follow-up effort by Bryant. Rudy canned two free throws for a 77-73 lead with 3:03 remaining.

Reserve forward Steve Shaw then blocked a Taylor jumper, but the ball wound up in Bryant's hand for an Explorer layup at the 2:54 mark. Then, Hackett took Lee's feed for an SU layup with 2:24 to go. Taylor countered for the Philly five from the 18-foot mark with 2:04 left.

With 1:42 left, Lee dribbled into the right corner against LaSalle's man-to-man defense. When he head faked, Bryant draped over SU's Mr. Outside. That finished Bryant—and Lee made both ends of a one-and-one for an 81-77 edge, which looked a little on the safe side.

However, the home team came right back again on a pair of Wise 18-footers, the last one knotting the count for the final time at 81-all, 53 seconds from the finish. SU finally put its sixth NCAA victory in 10 outings in the bag on a picture backdoor play, Hackett dropping a pass off to King for a layup with 35 seconds left on the clock. Wise tried for the equalizer, but his lane drive resulted in a turnover, Lee making the steal. And when Jimmy was fouled by 6-10 Donn Wilber (starting in place of injured Jim Wolkiewicz), he made both ends of a one-and-one for a four-point lead with 26 seconds to go.

55

With 16 seconds left, Wilber missed an eight-footer, the ball going over to SU. And three seconds later, frosh reserve guard Ross Kindel (who played 27 minutes) was fouled on a drive down the lane. He hit both ends of a one-and-one. That made Collier's answering layup meaningless.

SU's bench, as expected, had the edge. King and Kindel, particularly, outplayed a trio of reserves for LaSalle (a slim $1\frac{1}{2}$-point favorite).

Still, it was the play of seniors Hackett and Lee (7 of 14, six assists), plus junior Sease (8 of 11, mostly long-range bombs) which completed a night in which that Palestra jinx was shattered twice.

Late in regulation, however, it didn't look like SU would gain its fifth straight win on the Palestra hardwood. After 13 tie scores and 11 lead changes (Collier's 12-footer tying it at 71-all with 1:13 left), LaSalle gained possession after Lee's missed foul-line jumper and a near-miss tap-in. Twice the Explorers called time out, the final one with 15 seconds to go.

"When it gets to seven seconds," coach Paul Westhead told his Philly five, "let's drop it in low." And the Explorers wound up with the shot they wanted, a five-foot Bryant jumper from the left baseline. It rimmed the hoop, Hackett grabbing the rebound.

Danforth, having taken his club to its third straight NCAA tournament and fifth-consecutive postseason tourney, was a jubilant, cigarette-puffing winner. "We're pleased to be representing the ECAC in the Eastern Regionals and we're looking forward to playing North Carolina—a big club which (JV coach) Tommy Green was scouting in Charlotte."

Looking back at a frantic, always-close

RUDY HACKETT REBOUNDS.

game (SU's biggest lead was eight, LaSalle's four), Danforth said. "In the first half, we didn't do as well as we should defensively. They got the ball inside on us too easily (Bryant dominating, scoring LaSalle's first eight points, 17 at intermission)."

Westhead remarked that the Bryant short jumper was "the exact play we angled for." Then he added, "I think we played better (than when SU beat LaSalle, 82-78, earlier this season at Manley Field House). And so did Syracuse."

SU On Top

MARCH 21, 1975 | BY BOB SNYDER, SYRACUSE HERALD-JOURNAL

Providence, R.I.—Bill Orange's cagers are one win away from being cast in San Diego as Cinderella, Snow White and the Seven Dwarfs all wrapped into one make believe character.

That character would be challenging three other teams for the national collegiate basketball championship. The fantasy took a gigantic step toward reality as 10,981 disbelieving fans and a regional television audience saw Roy Danforth's Orangemen (22-7) put on a brilliant performance to topple a giant last night in the Providence Civic Center, as they nipped North Carolina, 78-76, in the NCAA East Regional semifinals.

It was the biggest win in Danforth's seven-year head coaching career at SU. Only historians dating back to the vintage years of the 1920s, when Syracuse reigned as national champion (selected in '26 by the Helms Foundation), could challenge the magnitude of this win over Dean Smith's sixth-ranked Tar Heels (22-8). A seven-point favorite, Carolina was an absolute choice of roundball experts to reach San Diego, where the final field of four will do combat March 29-31. Instead, the image of the ACC as the country's finest cage conference was tarnished when Jimmy Lee swished an 18-foot jump shot from left of the keyhole with five seconds remaining.

That shot tore through the heart of the ACC and cast 20th-ranked SU, now on an eight-game winning streak, against unranked Big Eight Conference runner-up Kansas State (20-8) in the East Regional title game.

In an evening of unlikely events, second-team All-American Rudy Hackett sat smiling in the corner of an Orange dressing room that bordered on hysteria. He'd been a non-factor in the offensive statistics. Yet SU had won one of the biggest—if not THE biggest—game in the school's 75-year basketball history.

"We're making a step now we've never made before," Hackett said. "There were probably only 17 guys in this whole place who thought we'd win . . . . Even a paper in neighboring Rochester said we were completely overmatched against North Carolina."

And while the Tar Heels were overplaying and double-teaming Hackett inside to the tune of just six points (his first sub double-figure scoring in 26 games) and a career low of one rebound, last night's drama unfolded as a 40-minute battle of the little men.

It was Lee and "Bug" Williams versus UNC southpaw Brad Hoffman and frosh sensation Phil Ford . . . . A war fought with long-range artillery . . . . Jump shots fired from as far as 25 feet away . . . . Lee delivered the last shot, leaving Carolina fatally wounded and sprawled on the floor at game's end, groping in futility for a ball rolling out-of-bounds . . . . Unable, after Williams made one of two free throws with two seconds remaining (making it

78-76), to fire one more time in a desperation bid for overtime.

The stage was set. Everyone but Syracuse's players and coaching staff read the script, which called for Carolina to roll through the regionals with a cast of characters including Hoffman, Ford (top performer in the ACC tourney), 6-9 Mitch Kupchak, 6-10ers Tommy LaGarde and Ed Stahl, 6-5 Walter Davis, a pressure defense that Williams quickly frustrated and a bench supposed to spit out the remains of Orange peels

THE SYRACUSE NEWSPAPERS

JIMMY LEE HITS THE GAME-WINNING SHOT AGAINST NORTH CAROLINA IN THE 1975 NCAA EAST REGIONAL SEMIFINALS.

on the Civic Center hardwood, where SU had fallen so hard in the second half just three months ago against the Providence Friars.

Carolina tested SU quickly, jumping out to a 6-0 advantage. And the Heels stepped it up to a pair of nine-point leads in the first half: SU was down. The KO punch was set for delivery. It never came—not until Lee, the nationally unheralded Orange co-captain from Windsor hit on his 12th of 18 shots.

While Lee's 24 points to lead SU was no surprise, sophomore Williams' career-high 19 points (9-for-11) was. So were the nine rebounds by 6-9 sophomore center Earnie Seibert, often the recipient of derogatory remarks because of being overweight, out of shape—averaging 4.6 for the 20-yard dash. But there they were, the strongest of a four-team Eastern field here that didn't figure in the first place. With Hackett unable to get the ball, then playing with four personal fouls, and with Nottingham product Chris Sease (10 points) giving it a go in his old size-12 sneakers,

despite an injured big toe, SU still won the big one.

They needed some solid bench play, and that came in spurts from Kevin King (12 points).

SU had come off the floor midway in the first half and closed to within one (42-41) at intermission. Carolina was shooting at a 67 percent clip, SU trying to stay with the taller Tar Heels and gunning with 56 percent accuracy.

"In the first half, we got absolutely nothing out of Hackett," said Danforth, who'll take his team into SU's third Eastern title game, the first since 1966 (under Fred Lewis), in a bid to reach the NCAA semifinals for the first time ever. "At halftime, I told myself, 'If we get nothing out of Hackett (who was averaging 22.6 ppg., 13.3 reebs), we've won the game.'"

But with 40 seconds left in SU's basketball season, Ford canned two free throws (his 10th in as many tries) to give Carolina a 76-73 lead. Sease kept SU alive with an 18-footer from the right side with 32 seconds left. And five seconds later, Ford's inbounds pass to LaGarde went out of bounds. Lee fired home the game-winner. Carolina called time out with three seconds left, then did so again before another tick of the clock.

Kupchak finally in-bounded as SU reserve center Bob Parker defended on the end line, the ball going OB to the Orange off Carolina sub Mickey Bell's hands. A second later, reserve Dave Hanners fouled Williams, who made one, then missed after another UNC time out.

Going for a loose ball, John Zaliagiris went sprawling, the ball rolling—and Syracuse was among the living in the NCAA's remaining armada, now sliced to eight.

SU had to shoot well, and they did (58 percent for the night, 35 of 60). Carolina was hotter—65 percent (32 of 49), Ford (7 of 10)

and Hoffman (10 of 12) scoring 24 and 20 points, respectively. The four starting backcourt players scored 87 points.

"Our team," said Danforth, "has had the attitude the last few years that if we stay close down the stretch, we can win. That doesn't always work out, however . . . . On our last basket, they had four people on Hackett. He just pitched it out to Jimmy for that nice little jumper . . . . This team has great character, attitude and poise (the latter gained following consecutive home losses to Rutgers and West Virginia, where leads of 16 and 21 points were wiped out) . . . . Our guards did a super job."

You're supposed to win 'em inside. But in an East Regional regarded by many as the lightweight of the four being played, five of six underdogs have been winners so far.

A pair of unlikely finalists remain, one soon to be winging to San Diego.

'snyde' remarks | m a r c h 2 1, 1 9 7 5

| by bob snyder |

Dean Smith said, "Williams, we understood, wasn't supposed to be a real good shooter. We gave him the room. And he proved us wrong . . . . When you lose 10 points to steals in the zone (SU's 2-3 zone), that's unheard of . . . . (Big Eight official) John Overby told Kuester, 'I blew it.' And I felt Kuester had drawn a foul on the last inbounds pass. But the refs didn't beat us, Syracuse did . . . . I don't think our four-corner offense hurt us—except that one charge by Ford (into Lee with 1:12 left, UNC up one, and upon which SU didn't capitalize). I think both teams played very well."

59

ON TO SAN DIEGO!

ORANGE IN NCAA SEMIFINALS

MARCH 23, 1975 | BY BOB SNYDER, SYRACUSE HERALD-AMERICAN

PROVIDENCE, R.I.—And then there were four . . . in San Diego.

In an historic moment in the Providence Civic Center, Jimmy Lee leaped into Rudy Hackett's arms, the joys of victory pulsating through this incredible Syracuse University basketball team, led by their two senior co-captains, and coached by Roy Danforth.

SU had just won the NCAA East Regionals for the first time in the school's 75-year cage history, defeating Big Eight Conference runner-up Kansas State, 95-87, in an overtime thriller before 9,295 fans and a national television audience. The victory puts the Orangemen, (23-7) winners of nine straight, into the NCAA final field of four, this Saturday (3:10 p.m. Eastern time against Kentucky) and the following Monday night (March 29-31)—something never done by an Orange five.

This battling bunch, thought by most everyone but the squad and coaches to be a loser in the semis against the East's top-rated North Carolina Tar Heels (SU won, 78-76), snatched a last chance for victory from the jaws of defeat when guard Jimmy (Bug) Williams motored up court past and through K-State pressure, then hit Hackett underneath.

Rudy bobbled the ball a second but recovered the handle in time for a left-handed layup over the front rim as the buzzer was sounding. There was no argument the shot had gone off before the buzzer, ending regulation even-stephen.

SU was still alive, the score tied at 76-76. And just eight seconds before, a 17-foot jump shot by K-State's brilliant guard, Chuckie Williams, had swished the cords from the left corner, seemingly making Jack Hartman's Wildcats (20-9) a winner.

K-State's Williams went on to score 35 points (tying his career high) and was selected the regional's most valuable player. He'd scored 32 in Thursday's 74-65 semifinal win over Boston College, who lost to North Carolina in yesterday's morning consolation character-builder, 110-90.

Hackett and Lee, plus Carolina's Brad Hoffman and Mitch Kupchak, joined Williams on the all-tourney team.

SU never trailed in overtime, Hackett giving the Orange a 78-76 edge with 4:29 left in OT, after taking a feed underneath from Lee, Williams countered for K-State at 4:03 on a drive down the right side of the lane. But it was Syracuse on top to stay when a Kevin King pass went to Hackett, then into "The Bug" for a layup from the left side of the hoop at the 3:47 mark.

The Orangemen, a 3 $\frac{1}{2}$-point favorite, went on to outscore the purple-clad Midwesterners, 13-3, for a certain victory (a 91-81 lead with 56 seconds remaining).

Hackett (10-for-21) led SU with 28 points and 16 rebounds, Lee (10-for-17) scoring 25, while Chris Sease added 12, "Bug" Williams and clutch sixth man King 10 apiece. Chuckie Williams' 35 (he was 14-for-27) was followed by backcourt mate Mike Evans' 20. But the frosh "Masked Marvel" hit on only 6-for-21, the two K-State starting guards tossing up 48 of the team's 84 shots, mostly long-range jumpers against SU's 2-3 zone.

SU shot 50 percent from the field (37-for-74), K-State only 41 percent (34-for-84). SU was on the short end in rebounding, 54-49, forward Dan Droge grabbing 18 caroms for the losers.

En route to SU's 19-11 overtime margin, Hackett dominated the defensive boards, limiting K-State to one shot. After SU went ahead to stay on Williams' layup Sease skied for one of his 10 reebs on a missed shot by K-State ace Williams. And Lee quickly popped in an 18-foot jumper from the middle of the keyhole for an 82-78 lead at the 3:20 mark. Then, Droge missed from the right corner for K-State, a team that fell short by one good inside shooter, "Bug" rebounded, was fouled, and canned both ends of a one-and-one for a six-point lead with 3:06 left in OT.

During a three-minute, 47-second span in which K-State, the Big Eight Conference runners-up, registered only one hoop from the field, it came on Chuckie Williams' 28-foot bomb from the right side. It was still a ballgame—84-80 with 2:29 on the clock. Williams was also fouled by the 'Bug', but missed the free throw. After two jump balls, Droge

missed inside, and the 5-10 "Bug" from Buffalo was there again for the reeb.

K-State reserve Bob Noland fouled out at 2:09, but Hackett missed the first of a one-and-one. However, King kept the ball alive for SU, and Sease scooped up the loose ball. The Orange were ready to sink the final nail into K-State's coffin, one which the Purple Wildcats had pried open twice in the first half. SU shook off early miscues to rip off nine straight points (three Lee jumpers and a Hackett three-point play) for an 18-9 lead.

Then, Chuckie Williams brought back K-State with a trio of long-range bombardments from the right side. Later, back-to-back steals by Lee and King produced a breakaway for frosh sub guard Ross Kindel and a Hackett layup (on a Kindel feed) for a 31-23 lead. But K-State registered its last 17 points of the first half from the backcourt (nine by Williams) for a 38-36 halftime lead over SU. The K-State guard duo extended its skein in the Wildcat scoring column to 23 in a row as SU fell behind, 44-38, early in the second half, before Sease and Hackett began to control matters.

That coffin lid was finally shut tight with 1:49 left in OT. That's when a give-and-go backdoor play on the right side saw Hackett feed Lee for a layup, Evans fouling out and Lee converting at the charity stripe for a three-point play . . . seven-point lead . . . and a Thursday morning flight to San Diego, California, for a yet tougher test Saturday against Southeastern Conference king Kentucky (25-4)—the Wildcat five who tamed previously unbeaten, No. 1-rated Indiana, 92-90, yesterday in Dayton.

Disbelievers were forced to become believers. Cinderella, Snow White and the Seven Dwarfs had turned fantasy into reality. Thousands of cheering Syracuse basketball fans, at Hancock Airport last night to greet the team's return flight, believe that the 20th-ranked Orangemen can perform another miracle.

61

ROY'S DREAM COMES TRUE!

MARCH 23, 1975 | BY BOB SNYDER, SYRACUSE HERALD AMERICAN

Providence, R.I.—There'll be something different when Roy Danforth heads for the National Championships later this week. He'll be taking a team with him!

"I've been going out there (to the NCAA cage championships) for 15 years . . . . I always told myself that someday I'd have a team here," said Danforth. "Now, I have one."

Danforth, the seven-year head coach at SU (his teams have won 128, lost 60), has done what no other Orange pilot could do—take a Syracuse basketball team to the Final Four. He recalled one of those earlier trips to the NCAAs. Without a team.

"I remember driving in an old, beat-up Studebaker from Hattiesburg, Mississippi, to Kansas City for the Nationals. I went with Lee Floyd, who was head coach at Southern Mississippi (Danforth's alma mater) where I was an assistant coach . . . . I told Lee that one day I'd be flying first class to the Nationals.

"Heck, I'm a young coach," continued the 39-year-old Danforth. "This is a dream of a lifetime . . . . It's been an unbelievable two weeks."

Unbelievable was the way in which SU fans would look back on what's happened—the way the Orangemen have surprised the roundball pundits by beating LaSalle in overtime, North Carolina, and now, Kansas State in overtime.

"It's great," said Danforth. "I think this is the greatest moment in Syracuse basketball history . . . . We're very, very proud to represent the East on the west coast . . . . And there haven't been too many eastern clubs in recent years outside the ACC (Atlantic Coast Conference) representing the East in the Final Four."

Danforth said he stuck with the things that had gotten SU this far. "But at the half, an adjustment we made was to try to spread our (2-3 zone) defense out a little wider, because they (K-State's Wildcats) were a better bunch of shooters on the move than standing still . . . . And Chuckie Williams is the best shooting guard we've seen."

Before SU's Jimmy (Bug) Williams motored in high gear to beat the clock, Danforth told his little speed merchant, "There's no question you've got all the time in the world. But we need a layup shot." And Rudy Hackett's layup was true.

"It's unbelievable how long five seconds is," added Danforth, who'll be in search of a high school gymnasium for SU's initial west coast drills on Thursday.

Danforth has no plans to change things against Kentucky. "We'll take it to 'em," said Danforth, who received a congratulatory telegram from his former cage boss at SU, Fred Lewis, now teaching at Sacramento State ("We were knocking on the door in '66. Hope you can go all the way.") . . . . And from County Executive John Mulroy, who declared Monday 'SU Basketball Appreciation Day' . . . And from Mayor Lee Alexander . . . . And a glad hand from Congressman Toby Moffett (SU, Class of '66) in the Hartford, Connecticut, airport en route home . . . . And those thousands of welcomes from SU fans at Hancock Airport.

It's hard not to believe in Orange basketball! Just one win away from joining the 1972-73 NCAA club (24-5) as the winningest in SU history, this history-making five is only two victories from the National Championship.

And as coach Roy added, "They even told me a man walked on water once."

'snyde' remarks | march 23, 1975

| by bob snyder |

This is SU's third-straight NCAAs, fifth ever. Marc Guley's 1957 team lost in Eastern finals to North Carolina, en route to Tar Heel national title. And Fred Lewis' 1966 team, led by superstar Dave Bing and SU assistant coach Jim Boeheim, bowed in Eastern finals to Duke . . . . SU goes to California following an 87-83 overtime win in Philly over LaSalle (after Explorer ace Joe Bryant missed five-footer at end of regulation), followed by Divine Providence—Lee's 18-footer with five seconds to go, sending ACC tourney-winning Tar Heels (favored to cop Eastern honors) back to Tobacco Road, while SU was to follow up with its third straight NCAA cardiac arrest as "Bug" beat the clock and Rudy gave the Orange another chance.

Hackett, Droge and Chuckie Williams went the 45-minute route. And in doing so, Hackett became SU's all-time single-season rebounder, his 389 surpassing Bill Smith's 378 in 1970-71 . . . . K-State center Carl Gerlach, a double-figure scorer before Eastern Regionals who scored 20, had 16 reebs vs. Penn, then tossed in 20 more vs. BC, was held scoreless (0-for-4) yesterday. The 6-10 pivot had only four reebs, was one of three K-Staters to foul out while SU fouled out its starting backcourt . . . . SU now 8-4 in NCAA play. K-State, 17th ranked and in its 12th NCAAs, has 17-16 record. In only previous meeting between schools, Danforth's first Orange team (1968-69) lost to K-State by 20 . . . . SU 0-2 vs. Kentucky, last meeting when Bing, Boeheim and Co. took a second-half licking in Lexington back in '64-65.

JIMMY LEE FALLS OVER FALLEN TEAMMATE RUDY HACKETT AND CHUCKIE WILLIAMS OF KANSAS STATE DURING THE 1975 NCAA EAST REGIONAL FINAL.

'CATS TOO WILD
FOR ORANGEMEN

MARCH 30, 1975 | BY BOB SNYDER, SYRACUSE HERALD AMERICAN

San Diego—We all knew it. The Impossible Dream had to end some time.

And it ended for Syracuse University's battling basketball team against the physically overpowering Kentucky Wildcats, who whipped SU, 95-79, in yesterday afternoon's NCAA Championship semifinal opener. Surprisingly, because the championships were a sellout, the crowd in the 15,200-seat Sports Arena was only 12,983.

The differences between Joe Hall's No. 2-ranked Wildcats (26-4) and Roy Danforth's sixth-rated Orangemen (23-8) were size, strength, muscle and inside depth. That's best manifested in rebounding, and the Southeastern Conference kings owned the boards, 57-40.

A "Drive For Five in '75," which had taken on an incredible new twist after SU gained its fifth-straight postseason tourney bid, third consecutive trip to the NCAAs, had been stopped by the nine-point favorites from the Bluegrass.

But the Orange did not quit, they did not get blown out and they showed they belonged with the best . . . the NCAA's final field of four, after winning their first-ever regional crown in thrilling overtime victories over LaSalle and Kansas State, sandwiched around that dramatic upset of Atlantic Coast Conference tourney champ North Carolina. What the game showed was that SU is still one or two players short.

Now, with that great pair of senior co-captains, Rudy Hackett and Jimmy Lee, ending their collegiate careers in Monday's consolation game against Louisville (before the UCLA-Kentucky title tussle), the need for a big recruiting year is now.

Kentucky, winner of six straight and in the finals for the first time since 1966 (when Baron Rupp's club lost to Texas-Western), started four seniors and one of three 6-10 freshmen centers (Rick Robey). But it was another frosh, 6-4 forward Jack Givens, who did the most damage for UK.

Givens, a southpaw like All-American teammate Kevin Grevey, led all scorers with 24 points (10-for-20) and shared rebounding honors with Robey (11 apiece). Givens, UK's third forward, was averaging just 9.0 ppg., but had come on strong late in the season. Grevey (only 5-for-13) scored 14, the backcourt of Jimmy Dan Conner and Mike Flynn (seven assists) had 12 and 11, respectively, 6-10 frosh sub center Mike Phillips adding 10.

65

Lee was the prime reason SU did not hit the floor and stay down. His outside shooting was spectacular. He hit on 6-for-8 after the Wildcats had taken a 44-32 halftime lead. That bulge was gained mainly on the strength of a four-minute, 47-second span midway in the half, in which UK went on a 13-3 spurt for a 32-20 lead while playing three frosh, a sophomore and senior.

High-flying Chris Sease, who couldn't get shots in the first half as Kentucky switched midway from a man-to-man to its 1-3-1 zone, scored 14 of his 18 points, had nine of his team-high 10 reebs in the last half. He shot 7-for-11 overall.

But Hackett, who played straight up while UK went man, took just three first-half shots. He wound up with 14 points, but had only five reebs—just the third time this season he failed to combine double-figure scoring with double-digit rebounding. Hackett was limited to 26 minutes of action because of foul trouble.

"Bug" Williams, Lee's backcourt mate who'd been hot in postseason play, had just four points (2-for-9), and seven turnovers in 23 minutes. Williams injured his right shoulder during the game, had it strapped and is questionable for Monday.

It was, in fact, a game unimpressively played by both clubs. And the Wildcats' performance shouldn't have scared UCLA, the perennial kingpin of collegiate basketball. The great effort by SU against Carolina in Providence was not to be yesterday.

Obviously disappointed, Danforth told the press after the defeat, "I read all week about UCLA, Kentucky, Louisville and 'who'. Well, I'm very pleased with our team. I think this is the best team in the history of Syracuse basketball."

'snyde' remarks | m a r c h   3 0,   1 9 7 5

| by bob snyder |

SU has never beaten Kentucky in three outings . . . . SU is 0-3 vs. Louisville . . . . Kentucky, seeking fifth national title in six NCAA finals, has always won semifinals upon reaching final four. And 'Cats, under Baron Rupp, defeated Wooden three times in only three games between the schools . . . . SU shot 52.9 per cent second half, 49.2 for the game. UK, after 51.4 first half, ended up 47.4. Wildcats had more than their share of breakaways . . . . SU now 8-5 in five NCAAs. Orange will have afternoon workout here today.

66

WOODEN SPEAKS SOFTLY BUT . . .

MARCH 30, 1975 | BY BOB SNYDER, SYRACUSE HERALD AMERICAN

San Diego—Were it not for a shoulder injury, a living basketball legend might have made his niche on the baseball diamond. "Baseball had always been my favorite sport," said the legendary John Wooden. "I was a shortstop. A pretty good one, they say. But I was hit in the shoulder . . . and that ended that.

"But I go to Dodger games all the time. Walter Alston is a very good friend of mine. I admire him a great deal."

That admiration cannot match, however, the elevated position in which Wooden is held by anyone connected with the sport of basketball. At a get-together hosted by *Sports Illustrated* the other night, the coaches of the four NCAA regional champs were on hand. But it was Wooden who drew the crowd.

And when he spoke in his soft, but firm voice, everyone listened . . . and by all, he was referred to with some reverence as "Coach."

Wooden's coaching statistics are well-known. They're also astounding. The former Purdue All-American guard has piloted 27 UCLA basketball teams with better than 80-percent success, copping nine national titles, seven in a row. His teams dominated the collegiate cage game in the 1960s and early '70s like no other school ever did.

And Wooden looks back on that '64 championship five—his first—as his favorite. "Comparatively speaking, it was the shortest of all NCAA champions . . . and it came closer to realizing its full potential than any team I have ever seen," Wooden said of the Walt Hazzard-Gail Goodrich-led team, without a player over 6-5.

Wooden's players maintain ties with their coach after leaving UCLA. "Lewis calls me when he's in Los Angeles," said Wooden of Lew Alcindor, now Kareem Abdul-Jabbar. "When I'm with him, I call him Kareem, out of respect. But I still refer to him as Lewis."

Wooden has been the center of conversation all year regarding who will be named his successor. But Wooden says of it all, "I won't have a hand in picking my successor—*when*—I retire . . . I don't feel it's my job, my place to do that . . . but I will go to UCLA games." Wooden announced his retirement after the Louisville game.

The fame that is solely UCLA's was described best by Wooden this way.

"I understand when Syracuse won the Regionals, there were thousands of fans at the airport . . . and the same, plus parades for Kentucky and Louisville, I believe . . . . When we arrived home at the airport, we were greeted by my wife, children and grand-children. And some players' wives.

"But winning is never matter of fact for me."

Regarding the coaching fraternity, Wooden feels the job done by Don Haskins at Texas Western in winning the NCAAs in 1966 (beating Kentucky) "was the best coaching job I've ever seen . . . for him to get those players to play disciplined basketball was remarkable."

It's a fact that Wooden refused the '76 Olympic Team coaching post before it was given to North Carolina's Dean Smith. "I don't want to talk about it." Wooden said politely. "Except to say, at one time I wanted the job."

Wooden expressed the desire for some rule changes (which will be discussed at rules committee and coaches' convention gatherings going on here. "I'm in favor of a 30-second clock," he said. "It was shown that even Hank Iba's teams (Oklahoma A & M) got the ball off in less than 24 seconds.

"And I'm for putting the dunk back in the game. Although I'm not so sure as I used to

THE SYRACUSE NEWSPAPERS

SU's 1974-75 Final Four team.

be. If the defensive man can't do what he wants (goal tend), why should the offensive man have that advantage?"

Asked about one of his great ex-players, Wooden said of Bill Walton, "He's physically strong enough for the pros . . . . No, I wasn't surprised about the problems he's had. He's more of a follower than a leader. He will listen, however."

And of an all-star five, Wooden said, "Lewis or Walton would be my MVP. But that's not necessarily the best player. It's the player who means the most to the team . . . Oscar Robertson (Cincinnati) is the best player I've ever seen. He could do more things than anyone else."

Orange Ends Great Year

PLAYS LOUISVILLE FOR 3RD PLACE

MARCH 31, 1975 | BY BOB SNYDER, SYRACUSE HERALD-JOURNAL

San Diego—It's been a very good year!

And who could have thought, in one's wildest imagination, in a Walter Mitty-like fantasy world, that the Syracuse University basketball team would end up rubbing shoulders—and elbows—with UCLA, Kentucky and Louisville? The same Syracuse team that couldn't win the ho-hum Kodak Classic and the team that dropped back-to-back home games to Rutgers and West Virginia after blowing big leads.

But Syracuse got here along with the giants of college basketball . . . carrying for the first time the banner of the East as its regional champion.

Why, of course it was a very good year. A great year. A first.

All of which points up the tremendously improved play of what is a rather young club—senior co-captains Rudy Hackett and Jim Lee notwithstanding . . . and the surprisingly unrecognized coaching job done by energetic Roy Danforth and his staff (Jim Boeheim, Tom Green).

There were many who felt Danforth was deserving of being named Coach of the Year in the East, which would have kept him abreast of his team (Number 1 in the East) and top inside man Hackett (the East's Player of the Year) . . . . And even some who felt the 39-year-old Orange skipper must have done the nation's best coaching job, bringing a club to San Diego for the 37th annual NCAA championships with 23 wins, on the heels of graduating two high pro draft selections (All-American Dennis DuVal, Fred Saunders) the year before.

Regardless, tonight ends what certainly was a surprise year, marked by some keen disappointments during the early and middle portion of the campaign. And more exciting, marked by a nine-game winning streak, including two easy wins in the new ECAC regional qualifier and three nail-biting NCAA victories, one of which was a shocking upset of ACC champ North Carolina. Such is not an everyday happening for Syracuse hoop fans.

It's a character-builder, the third-place consolation game against Midwest champ Louisville (27-3), a talented team led by Allen Murphy, Junior Bridgeman and Wesley Cox. The especially emotion-filled championship at 9:10 (Eastern time) pits No. 1-ranked UCLA (27-3), the West kingpin seeking its 10th title in the last 12 years under retiring coach John Wooden, against Joe B. Hall's No. 2-rated Mideast champs from Kentucky (26-4).

"Jimmy Lee was telling me at practice," Danforth recounted, "Coach, we can beat Louisville. They won't be up for this game.'"

That statement shows how much the Cardinals thought they could win it all. And it displays the character of this year's Syracuse club (23-8), one win away from equaling the 1972-73 NCAA team (24-5) for the most wins by an SU squad. Syracuse will be ready to play. But like Saturday, SU will enter the game on the short end, talent-wise and in the depth department.

Danforth, who'll head initially for Washington, D.C., and a few weeks of crucial recruiting starting Tuesday, discussed some highs and lows of the 1974-75 season:

"The beginning of the high was the George Washington game, when we were down, 12-0, and won (to start a nine-game victory streak snapped by Kentucky) . . . . Regardless of what we do against Louisville, we've played very well in the tournament, starting in Buffalo (ECAC vs. Niagara, St. Bonaventure), particularly against LaSalle, with great poise against Carolina and when we needed it against Kansas State. If we played against Kentucky the way we did against Carolina, I think we could have won.

"As a coach, it was a good year, because so many players learned to react properly at crucial times late in the season . . . . Individu-ally," added Danforth, "the most pleasant surprise—although he didn't play well Saturday—had to be 'Bug' (Williams, the speedy, 5-10 sophomore guard), who wasn't even a starter in the beginning of the season." His future now rests with academic work, specifically summer school sessions needed to remain eligible.

"The low has to be those two straight losses at home. It looked then," said Danforth, "like it could be a long year."

Happily, it proved to be longer than expected.

"No question," said Danforth, "the loss of Lee and Hackett (the latter being SU's No. 2 all-time rebounder, No. 3 career scorer) will hurt. Jimmy, in particular, has had a great tournament. The loss could be felt more in the backcourt, where Lee is by far the top scoring threat."

Although three starters and the top two reserves return, 1975-76 will have to receive somewhat of a rebuilding label. Hackett and Lee usually carried the club. Next year, it'll be "Rocket Man" Sease.

But Syracuse basketball fans won't forget this 1974-75 team, which made the "Drive For Five in '75" an exciting, memorable season.

Orange Comes Away With 'Glorious' Fourth

Louisville Wins, 96-88, in OT

APRIL 1, 1975 | BY BOB SNYDER, SYRACUSE HERALD-JOURNAL

San Diego—It reads, "1975 National Collegiate Championship, Fourth Place Team." A plaque doesn't tell the whole story of the stature in which Syracuse University basketball is now held across the country, following this 37th annual NCAA cage championship. Here, before a sellout crowd of 15,151 fans in the Sports Arena, Roy Danforth's sixth-ranked team missed upsetting 12-point favorite Louisville, rated No. 4, by a single bounce of a Jimmy Lee jump shot on the rim, losing in overtime, 96-88.

The whole thing was supposed to be meaningless. Just about everyone agrees consolation games decide nothing. Talent being equal, the team with character, pride in its performance and more desire to win will win. Syracuse, however, came to the NCAA's final field of four with a good deal less talent than UCLA, Kentucky and Louisville.

SU was Cinderella, Snow White and the Seven Dwarfs—who turned fantasy to reality in winning its first East Regional title, sending heavily favored North Carolina prematurely back to Tobacco Road. But now, it was San Diego . . . . The polls' No. 1-2-4 quintets . . . . And that club from the East, which had jumped from 20th to No. 6 in the AP ratings. The bumpkin was primed for the slaughter.

But the slaughter never came. Yes, SU lost Saturday to Kentucky by 16, but the Orange had rallied from 22 down to trail by nine with more than three minutes remaining. So, what was left, now that "The Impossible Dream" was over, now that the "Drive For Five In '75" had been halted? Now, there was Louisville, who had UCLA where they wanted 'em in the semifinals and let the Bruins off the hook. So while John Wooden waited in the wings to have his West Regional kings hand him a farewell gift, his 10th national championship in the last 12 years (with a 92-85 win over Kentucky), there was one more character-builder.

And when the biggest show in collegiate basketball came to an end, it was UCLA (28-3) on top of the heap again, followed by Kentucky (26-5), Louisville (28-3) and Syracuse (23-9). SU will drop in the final AP poll, of course. But to those who sat in on it all, they showed they belonged.

It was fitting that co-captains Rudy Hackett and all-tourney pick Lee would lead the Orange in their collegiate swan songs, with 28 and 27 points, respectively. But it was heartbreaking to see Lee's foul-line jumper, after he groped to find the handle on the ball and had to double-pump it up to the hoop. It bounced, bounced, bounced and just slid off the rim as the buzzer sounded, ending regulation at 78-all.

SU was to lose its first of the year in OT, after winning three—two of them NCAA thrillers. But in order to get to OT, the Orange had to overcome a horrendous shooting display (18.5 percent, 5-for-27) in the first 15 minutes, a 20-4 Cardinal streak that had SU on its knees (28-11) and scoreless for a 5:41 period, down by as many as 18 points, 16 at halftime (42-26).

"I guess some of our guys weren't ready to play," said a disconsolate Hackett. "But even Louisville—their guards were dying out there in the second half. I know I was tired . . . still, I'm in favor of playing consolations. I just like to play. It's a matter of pride. I don't want to go out and look bad."

Hackett's head slumped. He got an approving pat on the leg from Danforth . . . . And up walked a somber-faced Lee. "Thanks for everything, coach," he said, shaking hands with Danforth. It was the end of the Hackett-Lee era at Syracuse. It ended on a gutty, if disappointing note.

SU made Louisville's knees buckle with a second-half press and halfcourt trap, which caused 33 Cardinal turnovers. The Orange, down seven points with 6:05 left in regulation, ripped off eight unanswered points in a span of 1:05 to take its first lead, 66-65. Back and forth it went, SU up by three with 1:48 to go. But an Allen Murphy short jumper and Junior Bridgeman's 12-footer from the left side (on a three-point play) put SU down by two with 48 seconds left. With 37 seconds to go, Kevin King hit Hackett underneath from the right wing for the tying hoop. When Danny Brown missed a 10-footer with 15 seconds left, Hackett rebounded. "Bug" Williams missed a 10-footer with seven seconds left, Hackett latching onto the rebound again and passing it out to Lee at the foul line, the point from which Jimmy's game-winning bid did not fall.

In OT, Bridgeman ruled the roost with 12 of his 21 points. Bill Bunton led Denny Crum's Cardinals in scoring with 24, Murphy tossing in 20.

But SU, who'd lost center Earnie Seibert (sprained back) in the second half, finished up with Lee and the bench as Hackett, Williams and Chris Sease plus King fouled out in OT (along with Murphy). Louisville never trailed in OT (their second extra session here).

Bob Parker, who played very well as Seibert's backup, hit a foul-line jumper off the glass to put SU down, 90-88, with 1:03 left in OT. A Lee-Steve Shaw trap got SU the ball out of bounds. But Lee's in-bounder was picked off, Bridgeman was fouled and made both ends of the one-and-one. SU's final bid was a Lee jumper that missed, and the Cards added two hoops in the closing seconds.

"At halftime," Danforth said, "we talked about winning, character and pride. That it was the last game of the year. And the kids would have to live with it . . . . Now, they knew we were here."

And someday, somewhere, Syracuse will be back.

JIMMY LEE TOURNEY ALL-STAR

APRIL 1, 1975 | BY BOB SNYDER, SYRACUSE HERALD-JOURNAL

San Diego—Syracuse senior co-captain Jimmy Lee, who scored 50 points against Kentucky and Louisville here, was selected to the NCAA Championship's all-tournament team.

Lee was joined on the squad by Rich Washington (MVP) and Dave Meyers of champion UCLA, runner-up Kentucky's Kevin Grevey and Alan Murphy of Louisville.

Washington led all scorers with 54 points, 28 in the title game. Murphy had a total of 53 points, while Lee had 23- and 27-point efforts. Grevey had 48, including a 1975 tourney-high 34 last night. And Meyers wound up with 40 points.

'snyde' remarks | a p r i l 1, 1 9 7 5

| by bob snyder |

Hackett wound up with SU-record 412 reebs this season, second-best career total (995), third high in points for career (1,496) and season (709) . . . . Lee finished 11th in career points (1,165) and had 550 this season. He led SU in scoring during five-game NCAAs with 119 points, Hackett scoring 106 . . . . Full five shares of NCAA 32-team jackpot will net Orange over $100,000 . . . . SU outboarded by 17 each game here . . . . All players received NCAA watches . . . . SU arrives home at Hancock Airport at 9:20 tonight . . . . Danforth irked that Hackett, East's player-of-the-year, is not on 10-man East squad for annual East-West All-Star Game.

SU Cool in Stretch, Cops Crown

DECEMBER 4, 1977 | BY BOB SNYDER, SYRACUSE HERALD AMERICAN

For the first time since Jim Boeheim was playing the game on the Hill (1965-66), Syracuse University won a basketball tournament.

And they won it in a dramatic fashion that had the inaugural Carrier Classic capacity crowd of 9,546 under the Manley Dome on the edge of their theater-type seats.

It wound up SU 75, Michigan State 67 . . . . It was a heckuva lot closer than the final count of last night's championship affair.

The thriller actually was decided, as Classic MVP Earvin Johnson of the runner-up Spartans had predicted, on the boards. Rebounding, where statistically MSU had the final edge, 31-29. But the Orange won the battle of the trenches when it counted, in the final minute and 35 seconds with the score knotted at 63-all.

Sophomore guard Hal Cohen, who played superbly over 28 minutes, missed the front end of a one-and-one. But Orange teammate Marty Byrnes, who led the winners (4-1) with 18 points, eight reebs, swept the carom and was fouled . . . 1:34 left. Byrnes also missed the front end of a one-and-one.

This time, SU was not about to trust its free-throw shooting. "The Big Fella," as Boeheim calls 6-11 sophomore center Rosie Bouie, flew in to grab the rebound and drop it in the hoop.

And after Johnson's alley-oop pass misfired, Dale Shackleford grabbed the ball. The clock wound down inside a minute. Spartan guard Bob Chapman, whose 11-for-11 shooting fired MSU into the finals, fouled Cohen. The Canton Kid, whose schoolboy free-throw shooting exploits earned him a niche in the cage hall of fame, canned a pair in the one-and-one for a four-point lead.

In the final 41 seconds, it was Orange free-throw shooting against Johnson 20-footers. Bouie had a pair of one-pointers, answered by Johnson. Ross Kindle made two FTs, again answered by Johnson to make it 71-67 with 18 seconds left.

Six seconds later, Kindel canned another pair. And when Byrnes blocked Johnson's final bid, Cohen wound up with a breakaway layup to beat the buzzer.

MVP Johnson was joined on the all-tourney team by teammate Chapman, Jene Grey of LeMoyne, an 84-57 consolation game loser to Rhode Island, Bouie and Byrnes.

The MVP voting put a damper on what was a highly successful first-tourney venture

74

for Syracuse. Boeheim was infuriated.

"We've played in tournaments 15 straight years. Always, a player from the winning team is the MVP . . . . This is typical; it only happens in Syracuse.

"People say we're the best in the East and nobody (from SU) makes anything . . . . When Bing played on the West Coast, he had 40 and 38, and he didn't get MVP."

State coach Jud Heathcote agreed with Boeheim. "I always think the MVP trophy should go to a player from the winning team," Heathcote remarked. "Even if it's a guy who scores four points . . . somebody helped 'em win it."

Johnson was "Magic" opening night, something considerably less in the title game. He scored 12 points, hit only five of 14 shots, grabbed six reebs, had five assists, two steals, but also nine turnovers.

"I didn't expect it," the 6-8 State frosh said of the MVP vote. "I was surprised a guy from Syracuse didn't win it.

"The Syracuse team is great . . . . Those offensive rebounds on the free throws won it. And then they made those last six or seven free throws (eight to be precise)."

In addition to Byrnes and Cohen, other SU twin-figure production came from Bouie (14), Shackleford (13) and Louie Orr (12). Game-scoring honors went to MSU's burly rookie, Jay Vincent (23 on 10-for-14 shooting). Chapman added 15 but was only 3-for-10 from the field.

Grey led all tourney scorers with 49 points.

DALE SHACKLEFORD MAKES A REVERSE DUNK.

75

MICHIGAN STATE (67)

	fgm-fga	ftm-fta	r	a	tp
Keiser	4-7	0-0	3	1	8
Johnson	5-14	2-2	6	5	12
Vincent	10-14	3-3	6	0	23
Donnelly	1-3	0-0	3	1	2
Chapman	3-10	9-9	3	3	15
Charles	3-6	1-1	2	0	7
Feldreich	0-0	0-1	0	0	0
Bokovich	0-0	0-0	0	1	0
Team			8		
Totals	26-54	15-16	31	11	67

SYRACUSE (75)

	fgm-fga	ftm-fta	r	a	tp
Byrnes	6-10	6-7	8	2	18
Orr	6-8	0-0	6	0	12
Bouie	5-7	4-6	5	0	14
Kindel	0-1	4-4	0	2	4
Shackleford	6-14	1-1	2	3	13
Cohen	4-6	6-9	2	3	14
James	0-2	0-0	1	0	0
Schayes	0-1	0-1	1	1	0
Drew	0-1	0-1	1	1	0
Team			3		
Totals	27-50	21-28	29	12	75

statistics

Halftime—Syracuse 40, Michigan State 38; Personal fouls—Michigan State 26, Syracuse 18; Technicals Fouls—SU bench, Michigan State bench; Officials—Bellanti, Pavia

· ·

'snyde' remarks | d e c e m b e r 4, 1 9 7 7

| by bob snyder |

Orange shot well throughout, finishing with 54 percent from field. State was 56 percent last half, 48.1 for game . . . . All seven blocked shots were by Orange defenders (three by Bouie) . . . . Byrnes, Johnson went 40-minute route . . . . State had 21 turnovers, SU only 14.

SU came up with seven steals, State six . . . . SU, State 6-6 over years. This was first meeting since '46-47 . . . . Orange, ranked 12th nationally prior to this week's play (three wins, one loss), next in action Wednesday at Colgate.

HONEYMOON'S OVER!
ORANGE OUSTED

MARCH 15, 1980 | BY BOB SNYDER, SYRACUSE HERALD-JOURNAL

Philadelphia—Syracuse really isn't the Beast of the East. They're not even the Georgetown of the East.

But then again, neither is Maryland the UCLA of the East.

The fact is the best Orange basketball team of 'em all has packed it in for another season . . . A season with more promise than any that preceded it. The one that was extinguished in last night's NCAA East Regional semifinals by a 9-0 Iowa spurt, keyed by a technical called on SU coach Jim Boeheim.

The Orange, a two-point favorite, had been flush with a six-point lead. The damage left SU down three, flat, and headed toward an 88-77 termination of its third 26-win campaign in a four-year Boeheim-coached tenure that's produced a nationally unprecedented 100 wins and a 3-4 NCAA record.

For the third time, the end came in the Regional semifinals. The Sweet Sixteen has been SU's limit—since the Final Four year of '75.

The fact the Orange (26-4) was the No. 1 East seed meant nothing to the Hawkeyes (22-8), fourth in the Big Ten and the No. 5 seed (no bye). Georgetown (26-5), possessor of the nation's longest winning streak (15) and previous winner over No. 2-seed Maryland (24-7), let alone two-time winner over SU, didn't play like a No. 3 seed in ending Lefty Driesell's season, 74-68, in last night's afterpiece, before 17,569 at the Spectrum.

Nor will they on Sunday, when they beat the Hawkeyes and earn a berth in the Final Four, March 22-24 in Indianapolis.

Where did SU go wrong this time? In a number of areas . . . . The folks who played in the backcourt, other than Eddie Moss, went 1-for-14 for starters. And they always say SU's guards take them so far, then drop them off in the NCAAs.

Certainly, Marty Headd's 0-for-7 was damaging.

"Marty's had a great year," said Boeheim. "He just didn't make 'em. It's that simple."

His shots weren't going. In the first half—the first 10 minutes of which saw SU operating with a nonexistent attack—Headd's shots were forced.

"I had good shots," the CBA product felt. "I wanted to get going in the second half. But I just kept hitting back iron."

"All year long, the guards were consistent," said Boeheim. "We certainly got nothing out of 'em tonight."

Iowa's man-to-man defense played its role. But guard Hal Cohen felt SU had been up against better defensive teams.

The backcourt was only part of the problem. After all, the Ronnie Lester-Kenny Arnold Hawkeye tandem was only 5-for-17, Lester's containment owing to Moss' defensive prowess and Lester's having to play on less than two healthy legs.

There was Roosevelt Bouie, the 6-11 defensive stopper. He was on the court just 19 minutes. His 18 points, backing Louis Orr's brilliant 25-point, 16-rebound, eight-assist performance, looks good on the stat sheet.

"Rosie played a great game, when he was in there," said Orr, who scored all his points the last 23 minutes. But Bouie's absence for 21 minutes was felt more than his presence.

"Roosevelt played as good as he has all year long," said Boeheim.

Strangely, Bouie ran into late-season foul trouble he'd rarely been plagued with the three previous months. But in the last seven games, he averaged just 22 minutes playing time and less than five rebounds.

Even Orr's effort couldn't overcome that.

Still, there was the Orange, down (by seven) at halftime, the 10th time they'd trailed at intermission. Eight of the previous nine times, the Orange survived at the end.

The Hawkeyes, while unbeaten outside the Big Ten, had seen four of its eight losses come as the result of blown halftime leads.

"It was a game of spurts," said Hawkeye coach Lute Olson. "And after halftime, Syracuse came out better prepared than us, much better prepared." To the tune of a 10-0 run, following an opening basket by Vince Brookins, who led a five-man double-figure assault with 21 points (11 of 12 from the foul line, where the Hawks canned their last 14 when SU played catchup down the stretch).

And when Moss intercepted a pass to set up an Orr stuff, SU went ahead, 57-51, just 8:29 away from the Elite Eight.

"We were playing stupid ball at that time," suggested Iowa's Kevin Boyle (18), the 40-minute man and all-purpose performer.

"But we kept our character, our intensity on defense. Usually, we break down."

It was SU who would break down.

After Boyle rebounded his own shot, rookie Erich Santifer drove the left side and collided with Brookins. The contact meant nothing to Brookins, who'd broken two legs when hit by a car as an eight-year-old and survived open heart surgery following a race riot-stabbing as a 10th grader.

Nor did it mean anything to the officials, who called Santifer for charging, that there also might have been goaltending on the shot.

Then Lester dragged one in from the lane and it was 57-55.

When rookie Tony Bruin fouled Brookins under SU's board, Boeheim was on his feet; gesturing.

Pac-10 official Booker Turner slapped Boeheim with a technical (two shots), nothing new to the Orange coach in the late stages of this season.

Brookins made both ends of a one-and-one and one-of-two technical tosses, giving Iowa a one-point lead 7:16 from the end.

Possession produced a bank off the glass by center Steve Krafcisin (14) with 6:59 left . . . . A five-point play . . . . SU's plus-six was minus-three with 90 clicks of the clock.

Boeheim didn't deserve the technical. But with the lead in the latter fourth of the game, neither should you even give an official a chance to quick whistle you.

"I was just talking to Tony Bruin. I told him not to reach," said Boeheim. "I stayed in the bench area . . . . I'd been up the whole game. He didn't warn me.

"I'm sure he (Turner) thought I was talking to him, but I didn't. I didn't believe it."

"We were making a run at that time," said Olson. "I felt we'd have gotten 'em anyway."

"I thought it was the key to the game," said Boyle.

"The key," said Boeheim, "was inside. With Bouie out of there (5:25 from the finish, SU in a catchup role), they got too many second shots."

"It was a very, very key play," Headd said of the technical.

"It was a big swing of points," added Cohen. "It might have been the incentive for them. They could say, 'We could win this game.' "

"It was a drop. But there was time on the clock and we'd been in the hole before," said Moss.

To Orr, "It was sort of bursting the bubble."

ROOSEVELT BOUIE IN ACTION.

MARK DEANGELI, THE SYRACUSE NEWSPAPERS

SU was only one down on two Bouie free throws, then a Bouie layup on an Orr feed (62-61 with 6:04 left).

Brookins, Arnold (12) and Steve Waite (10) extended the lead, mostly from the charity stripe.

Another Syracuse basketball season was history.

Once again, the Orange—who'd aroused more Upstate fever than any predecessor—was just its old NCAA instant replay.

Disappointment would, for some, overshadow the accomplishments at Purdue and St. John's . . . . And the No. 6 national ranking that at one point reached Avis proportions.

For some, only the last game is remembered. Like North Carolina-Charlotte, Western Kentucky and Pennsylvania.

This season that seems unfair. Yet, this season wasn't going to end this early, this way.

Corn Grows Tall
game summary | march 15, 1980

IOWA (88)

	fgm-fga	ftm-fta	reb	ast	tp
Brookins	5-10	11-12	5	2	21
Boyle	8-12	2-2	5	0	18
Krafcisin	6-9	2-2	3	1	14
Lester	3-10	3-5	3	7	9
Arnold	2-7	8-13	5	5	12
Hansen	1-2	2-2	1	3	4
Waite	4-5	2-3	5	0	10
Team rebounds			4		
Totals	29-55	30-39	31	18	88

SYRACUSE (77)

	fgm-fga	ftm-fta	reb	ast	tp
Santifer	5-9	4-4	3	1	14
Orr	10-17	5-5	16	8	25
Bouie	7-8	4-5	3	0	18
Moss	4-7	0-0	1	3	8
Headd	0-7	0-0	3	3	0
Bruin	1-5	0-0	3	2	2
Cohen	0-2	0-0	1	2	0
Schayes	2-7	6-9	2	1	10
Team rebounds			5		
Totals	29-62	19-23	37	20	77

Halftime Score: Iowa 40, Syracuse 33
Personal fouls: Iowa 20, Syracuse 28
Fouled out: Krafcisin, Bouie, Moss
Technical foul: Boeheim
Officials: Paul Galvan (SEC), Dale Kelley (SEC),
Booker Turner (Pac-10)
Attendance 17,569.

PETER HALPERN, THE SYRACUSE NEWSPAPERS

PEEKABOO! MARTY HEADD
LOOKS FOR A FRIENDLY FACE.
HEADD PLAYED FOR SYRACUSE
FROM 1977-1981.

80

Red-hot, pulse-pounding basketball...Syracuse style!

A winning tradition...SU Basketball and Time Warner Cable.

Throughout the history of the Dome, many great games come to mind for all of us. As a member of the community, Time Warner Cable and its employees are proud to have witnessed the thrills of Syracuse University Basketball.

We've been right there with you, bringing you the games on cable TV or on our very own local programming networks.

It's our way of saying thanks to our customers, the fans, and for the great tradition of SU Basketball.

TIME WARNER
CABLE

LEO RAUTINS

Leo Rautins (11) watches his game winning tip-in. The Orangemen take the Big East title from Villanova.

PHOTO CREDIT: DAVID LASSMAN

PEARL WASHINGTON

JANUARY 21, 1984

The Syracuse bench explodes with joy as guard Dwayne "Pearl" Washington sinks a half-court shot at the buzzer to beat Boston College in the Carrier Dome.

PHOTO CREDIT: JIM COMMENTUCCI

JIM BOEHEIM

MARCH 21, 1987

Syracuse University's Jim Boeheim after a win over North Carolina at the Meadowlands.

PHOTO CREDIT: STEPHEN D. CANNERELLI

RUMBLE!

MARCH 28, 1987

Stevie Thompson, coach Jim Boeheim, and Rony Seikaly try to break up a tussle between Syracuse University's Derrick Coleman and Providence College's David Kipfer as another fight erupts nearby. Syracuse would go on to win, 77-63, sending it to the NCAA finals.

PHOTO CREDIT: HARRY DiORIO

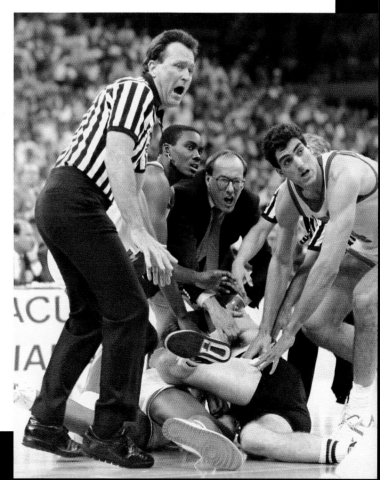

DEJECTION!

Only one team wins its last game and (left to right) Rony Seikaly, Derrick Coleman, Greg Monroe and coach Jim Boeheim try to deal with the Orangemen's 74-73 loss to Indiana.

PHOTO CREDIT: HARRY DIORIO

BILLY OWENS

MARCH 4, 1990

Syracuse forward Billy Owens, fouled with one second remaining in regulation, tosses in two free throws to tie the game and force overtime against Georgetown.

PHOTO CREDIT: HARRY DIORIO

JASON CIPOLLA

MARCH 22, 1996

Syracuse University's Jason Cipolla hits a shot to send the game into overtime against Georgia at an NCAA Tournament game in Denver.

PHOTO CREDIT: STEPHEN D. CANNERELLI

TODD BURGAN

MARCH 24, 1996

Syracuse University's Todd Burgan catches an alley-oop pass against Kansas in NCAA Tournament action at Denver.

PHOTO CREDIT: STEPHEN D. CANNERELLI

JOHN WALLACE

MARCH 24, 1996

Syracuse University's John Wallace celebrates after the Orangemen's victory over Kansas.

PHOTO CREDIT: STEPHEN D. CANNERELLI

JOHN WALLACE & TODD BURGAN

MARCH 30, 1996

Syracuse University's John Wallace (44) lets out a shout in celebration of the Orangemen's win over Mississippi State at the Meadowlands.

PHOTO CREDIT: STEPHEN D. CANNERELLI

SYRACUSE FANS

MARCH 30, 1996

Mayhem breaks out on Marshall Street as fans celebrate Syracuse University advancing to the NCAA Basketball Final Four Championship game.

PHOTO CREDIT: SUZANNE DUNN

JOHN WALLACE

APRIL 1, 1996

John Wallace shoots over Kentucky's Antoine Walker in 1996 NCAA Tournament action.

PHOTO CREDIT: STEVE PARKER

SYRACUSE ORANGEMEN

APRIL 1, 1996

Syracuse University's Orangemen pull together after John Wallace fouled out in an NCAA basketball title game at the Meadowlands.

PHOTO CREDIT: STEPHEN D. CANNERELLI

LAZARUS SIMS & TRAINER DON LOWE

APRIL 1, 1996

Syracuse guard Lazarus Sims and trainer Don Lowe walk with bowed heads toward the Continental Arena locker room after the NCAA basketball title game at the Meadowlands.

PHOTO CREDIT: STEPHEN D. CANNERELLI

TONY "RED" BRUIN HANGS
ON THE RIM, EXPECTING A
TECHNICAL FOUL CALL.

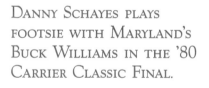

MARK DEANGELI, THE SYRACUSE NEWSPAPERS

DANNY SCHAYES PLAYS
footsie with MARYLAND'S
BUCK WILLIAMS IN THE '80
CARRIER CLASSIC FINAL.

81

THE SYRACUSE NEWSPAPERS

SYRACUSE BASKETBALL: A CENTURY OF MEMORIES

Orr Glistens in Final Hour

MARCH 15, 1980 | BY BOB SNYDER, SYRACUSE HERALD-JOURNAL

Syracuse's most qualified team to make it to the Final four had not made it.

Not even to the regional finals, in the city where they'd won seven straight times and not lost in seven years.

This time SU rolled craps. But not because of Louis Orr, the kid who'll always be remembered as the skinny forward from Cincinnati. The player nobody wanted and the one many opposing coaches most feared.

For the last time, he had been the guy who wasn't gun-shy when the Orange needed guns desperately. His 25 points (10-for-17), 16 rebounds and eight assists might not be remembered on Salina Street.

Neither would the 1,462 points that came before.

What the Louie half of Bouie 'n Louie meant to Syracuse's basketball program could not vanish with a loss, even another bitter NCAA pill that had to be swallowed.

Jim Boeheim's technical, albeit undeserved, would be remembered for the damage it did.

"It (the 'T') didn't matter," said Boeheim, whose 100 wins in his first four years are a record, although the NCAA keeps no such figures.

"The next three times down the court, we forced the ball inside," added Boeheim. If that lead had not vanished so quickly, perhaps SU wouldn't have been so flushed.

But that's all conjecture. And history. Like the Orange careers of Orr, Roosevelt Bouie and Hal Cohen, all those Manley wins and 100 successes on various courts in 118 contests.

It ended—as it does for all but one team—in disappointment.

"I still know we're a great team," said Bouie, SU's No. 2 all-time scorer (1,560), after being whistled down for the final time. "Our record (26-4) proves it. Deep down, I still know it."

Such knowledge did not deter Iowa.

"The beginning of the second half, we played our best basketball of the year," Cohen felt.

"It'll be kind of strange," added Cohen,. "Some of the guys will be back. They can say, 'We can get 'em next year.'

"But for Roosevelt, Louis, and myself, there's no next year . . . . I think they'll have great pro careers. I'll have to wait for the draft," said the future doctor, kiddingly, trying to make light of a dark day.

Louis Orr would smile. "To me, it was my favorite year, a lot of fun . . . . The people I met, the friendships—real good friends like my roommate, Eddie (Moss).

"I felt good about this team, on the court and off. They were always in my corner; I loved that. And I was in theirs.

"I'm disappointed," Orr went on, "to come so close and fall short (a late foul-line parade disguising the fact SU was still close two minutes from season's end). But, I'm not disappointed in our performance.

"We gave it our best."

Orr's best left Iowa and more than 15,000 Spectrum fans understandably impressed.

BOUIE AND LOUIE (55) IN UNISON.

What SU had to give was felt by some to be sufficient to warrant the Final Four trip to Indianapolis. Whatever was given was not enough, however.

"We were getting the breaks all year long," said Dan Schayes, who can say, 'Wait till next year.'

"But I thought this year was a little special."

It was.

EDDIE MOSS (WITH BALL) VERSUS GEORGETOWN IN THE '79-80 SEASON.

SU Takes Title in Real Thriller

Rautins MVP

MARCH 8, 1981 | BY BOB SNYDER, SYRACUSE HERALD AMERICAN

Leo Rautins had just climbed as high as he could off the Demi Dome floor. His tip-in of Erich Santifer's missed 12-footer with three seconds remaining in the third overtime period would give Syracuse a victory virtually beyond description in yesterday's Big East Tournament championship . . . . This had been a tip-in with a ninth consecutive NCAA Tournament bid written all over it.

Villanova would lock itself out of its final chance for yet another extra session by calling a timeout, when the Wildcats had none remaining.

Dan Schayes would ice the cake with a free throw, ending what was perhaps the greatest collegiate basketball game played in this town, the final count being 83-80.

And there was Rautins, the Canadian kid told by doctors at age 11, following back surgery, that his greatest physical activity would be walking. Now, Leo Rautins was walking tall, scanning the uppermost reaches of the Demi Dome for his parents. The 6-8 sophomore forward from Toronto, home at last in an Orange uniform after beginning collegiately at Minnesota, had made a deal with his folks.

"Come to the tournament on Saturday; we'll be in the finals," he'd told his father.

Rautins searched. It was goalie Jim Craig, draped in the American flag, seeking out his dad.

"I was trying to see where they were," said Rautins, whose 16 points and 11 rebounds was but one part of the remarkable, three-day Orange success story, all the more impressive because of the loss of zone-breaking guard Marty Headd.

"I found 'em in the stands . . . . They were kinda jumping up and down."

So were thousands of fans who half-filled the Demi Dome in body, but totally filled it vocally. The paid gate was 15,213 and announced turnstile count 13,477—diminished by NBC's live television cameras.

Statistically, Jim Boeheim's Orangemen (18-11) were as impressive as they were on the court during three days that included earlier wins over St. John's and Georgetown. SU shot well (59 percent), rebounded unlike a team that had been outboarded during the season (owning the glass, 38-21) and showed a maturity that reared its head at the proper moment.

Rollie Massimino's Wildcats (19-10)—perhaps hanging by a proverbial limb with the Hoyas for what could be one of three NCAA bids tendered today to Big East teams—shot 53 percent. They were an awesome 70 percent after halftime.

Tony "Red" Bruin led all scorers with 22 points, fouling out in the first overtime. Santifer netted 18, Schayes adding 15 and 11 caroms. 'Nova, last year's Eastern Eight champ and survivor of OT against Providence on Friday after beating Connecticut, was led by Alex Bradley (21) and John Pinone (19). Stewart Granger (14), Aaron Howard (11) and Tom Sienekiewicz (10) were also in double-figures for the 'Cats, who'd beaten SU twice in regular-season play.

In addition to MVP Rautins, the all-tourney team included Orange teammates Santifer and Bruin, plus Bradley and Pinone, and Georgetown's Eric "Sleepy" Floyd.

This second annual cagefest attracted a paid gate of 53,505—20,000 more than last year's inaugural in Providence—and cleared gross ticket sales of $50,000. An extra $60,000 of TV money sweetens the conference pot.

It didn't look sweet for the Orange late in the first OT. In a game in which the teams never separated by more than six points, SU trailed, 70-64, with 2:18 left.

Eddie Moss, whose floor play was all-tourney caliber throughout, hit from the lane. Bruin fouled out at 1:42, Pinone missing the front end of a one-on-one. Moss' inside feed for a Schayes layup cut the gap to two inside the 90-second mark.

After an SU timeout, Santifer gambled and won. You had to play like it was a crap shoot, because this young league (won in regular-season play by Boston College) was a crap shoot from top to bottom.

LEO RAUTINS' TIP-IN TO WIN THE 1981 BIG EAST TOURNAMENT TITLE IN THREE OVERTIMES VS. VILLANOVA IS ONE OF THE MOST FAMOUS BASKETS IN SU HISTORY.

Santifer picked Sienkiewicz' pocket, but missed a two-footer. Moss tipped it in for the equalizer with 76 seconds left.

Nova bled the clock, but wound up with Granger's 30-footer bounding off the front rim.

"That first overtime, when we were down six, was probably the first time I ever thought we were out of a game," admitted Boeheim. "But our kids found a way—somehow."

"I'm not disappointed in the coach, that he thought we were out of it," said Santifer. "He'll know better next time."

SU, unable to shake free of the 'Cats after breaking out to an immediate 8-2 lead and up two at intermission, appeared to win it in regulation. Before the midway point of the second half, the Orange went to a spread offense and did go up by six, 51-45.

"We didn't want to play against their zone the second half," said Boeheim. "And every time we got the lead, they made a jump shot (Bradley leading the Wildcat effort from long range).

Ahead by one with 1:04 left and Moss on the line, SU apparently had applied the clincher with two made free throws on a one-and-one. But Rautins was called for entry into the lane before Moss finally let his second shot go.

SU had a two-point lead, rather than three. Bradley's foul-line jumper with 20 clicks left tied it. Rautins' rushed 20-footer with :06 left gave 'Nova a desperation last shot.

Sienkiewicz' 30-foot, back-to-the-basket, over-the-shoulder hook went off the rim . . . . It was dramatic, but would not have counted had it gone in.

Fifteen more minutes of drama remained.

"We had so many opportunities," said Boeheim. "All the opportunities."

SU led by four in OT No. 2, when Schayes turned and drove the lane for a dunk,

then made a one-and-one for a 78-74, led with 1:06 to go. Sienkiewicz' 20-footer with 18 seconds to go knotted it at 78.

Santifer's 15-footer missed. Moss' short follow going around and out . . . . OT No. 3 was next.

'Nova was in its second OT game in as many days, SU its first in a season that included the most losses since 1969-70, a sixth-place Big East finish and 10 losses in the last 18 games prior to the tournament.

The Orange would be written off by some. Not now.

Schayes made two FTs in a one-and-one situation, but Granger's bomb tied it at 80. SU worked the clock the final minutes before calling timeout with eight seconds left. When Santifer missed, Rautins did not.

"That last tap was a super one, over Aaron Howard," said Massimino. "That's college basketball."

Yesterday was college basketball at its best, Big East style.

"I made the mistake," he said of the timeout producing the game-ending technical. "That's the first time I ever did that in 25 years of coaching.

"I saw Leo Rautins on the baseline. We wanted to run a trick play and draw a foul."

When the 'T' was called, Granger knew it was over.

"I couldn't believe it. I knew we'd lost the game . . . . I thought we had 'em in that first overtime," said the 'Nova point guard.

So did Boeheim.

Santifer and a bunch of Orangemen who gambled and won proved him wrong.

ERICH SANTIFER WAS A PIVOTAL PLAYER IN SYRACUSE'S TRIPLE OT WIN OVER VILLANOVA IN THE BIG EAST TOURNAMENT CHAMPIONSHIP.

86

DON'T ENVY GAVITT

MARCH 8, 1981 | BY BOB SNYDER, SYRACUSE HERALD AMERICAN

The guy who wears so many hats—Big East commissioner, successor to Wayne Duke as NCAA basketball committee chairman, Providence athletic director—has had a busy weekend.

Some Big East member institutions will know how much weight he was able to throw around in Kansas City when the 48-team NCAA tournament field is announced this afternoon.

"He'll earn his pay," conceded Syracuse coach Jim Boeheim, after his team beat Villanova in the most remarkable game these eyes have witnessed in 15 years of covering collegiate roundball.

SU's 83-80 DemiDome victory over Villanova in triple overtime gave the Orange the Big East crown, one they couldn't wear after winning 25 of the first 27 games a year ago in Providence.

With it, there was no guaranteed NCAA bid. Merely the likelihood of an at-large berth. And then, not necessarily in the East Regional—Thursday and Saturday in Providence, Friday and Sunday in Charlotte.

SU needed to win the tourney on its own tartan court or it was NIT, here we come.

It would be shocking if the phone call doesn't come from the NCAA, particularly after eight such calls have previously come in succession. Only UCLA and Marquette can make that statement.

Regular-season champ Boston College (21-6), KO'd here in round one by last-place Providence, appears an NCAA lock.

SU (18-11) hadn't lost so many times since Roy Danforth's second year. But the Orange won the battle of the boards on successive occasions against St. John's, Georgetown and 'Nova. They found the required zone-breaking lost by Marty Headd's pre-tourney broken wrist in the outside shooting of MVP Leo Rautins and Erich Santifer. They played intelligent, aggressive basketball worthy of inclusion in the NCAAs.

Then there's the Philly Wildcats (19-10), who were 5-6 during star forward Alex Bradley's 11-game injury absence . . . . And Georgetown (20-11), with All-American guard "Sleepy" Floyd, who lost here in the semifinals to SU. The Hoyas, a bucket away from last year's Final Four, were second in conference regular-season play and their schedule began against heavyweights at the Great Alaskan Shootout.

Connecticut, St. John's and one of the teams falling short of an NCAA invite can be expected to form a trio bound for the NIT.

The Big East, completing its second year, will not gain automatic entry to the NCAAs until next season; the conference is at the mercy of the selection committee.

Gavitt is a heavyweight among that group. With so many conference tourney upsets placing otherwise unpicked teams into automatic berths, the at-large portion of the field narrows.

To think the Big East will receive more than three berths (the number gained a year ago) is suggesting the league is more than it currently is.

A year ago, the NCAA computerized Rating Percentage Index (RPI) had the Big East ranked No. 1 among conferences. That's not the case this year, where the Top 20 wire service rankings do not include any Big East teams.

So this morning comes the wait. In Syracuse, the wait should be worth it.

And with one phone call will come the word, be it a junket to Providence or Charlotte, Dayton or Tuscaloosa (Mideast), Austin or Wichita (Midwest), Los Angeles or El Paso (West).

It will be a trip a lot of people, just a few days ago, never thought Syracuse would be making.

game summary | march 7, 1981

VILLANOVA (80)

	fgm-fga	ftm-fta	r	a	pts
Howard	5-6	1-1	3	0	11
Bradley	8-15	5-6	2	0	21
Pinone	7-14	5-6	7	0	19
Granger	7-11	0-0	3	3	14
Sienkiewicz	4-10	2-2	2	4	10
Mulquin	1-3	1-1	2	0	3
Dobbs	1-3	0-0	0	1	2
Team			2		
Totals	33-62	14-16	21	8	80

SYRACUSE (83)

	fgm-fga	ftm-fta	r	a	pts
Rautins	8-16	0-0	11	2	16
Bruin	11-13	0-0	4	0	22
Schayes	5-8	5-6	11	7	15
Moss	3-5	3-3	2	6	9
Santifer	9-17	0-0	0	2	18
Waldron	1-3	1-2	3	2	3
Kerins	0-1	0-0	0	0	0
Team			5		
Totals	37-63	9-11	38	19	83

Halftime: Syracuse 35, Villanova 33. Regulation: Syracuse 62, Villanova 62. First OT: Syracuse 70, Villanova 70. Second OT: Syracuse 78, Villanova 78. Personal fouls: Villanova 16, Syracuse 15. Fouled out: Bruin. Technical foul: Villanova (illegal timeout). Officials: Jody Sylvester, Larry Lembo, Mickey Crowley. Attendance: 15,213 (paid), 13,477 (turnstile).

statistics

GENE WALDRON AND RAF ADDISON PLAYED FOR SYRACUSE IN THE MID '80s. WALDRON (ABOVE) RECEIVED THE 1984 CARRIER CLASSIC MVP AWARD AFTER HIS RECORD 40-POINT GAME. ADDISON (RIGHT) SHOOTS A JUMPER OVER PITT'S CHARLIE SMITH IN 1985.

PEARL'S SHOT BEHEADS HOYAS

32,229 FANS REJOICE IN 65-63 WIN

JANUARY 29, 1985 | BY BOB SNYDER, SYRACUSE HERALD-JOURNAL

On a Monday evening when fruits and nuts came out in force, The Shot did everything but bring the roof down on the Carrier Dome floor.

Dwayne Washington's 15-foot foul-lane jumper with eight seconds remaining did everything else.

It transformed a one-point deficit into a one-point lead and an eventual 65-63 victory for No. 8-ranked Syracuse University (13-3), it sent No. 2 Georgetown (18-2) down to its second defeat in three days, it turned the Big East into a logjam back of St. John's, and it produced a dangerous state of delirium among many of the 32,229 fans.

"They cleared the side out for me," said Washington. "The decision (during a timeout with 16 seconds left) was for me to go one-one-one, everybody else crash the boards. I had to go, because time was running down.

"I knew I couldn't go all the way. It was clogged, and I didn't want to get an offensive foul. It was a little further away than I wanted. But it just so happened that the basket went and everybody didn't have to crash the boards."

The same backboard had been crashed just 2 $\frac{1}{2}$ minutes into the game by a nut hurling a fruit. An orange splattered against the glass as Hoya center Patrick Ewing missed a free throw. Officiating crew chief Hank Nichols awarded Ewing another first shot of a two-shot foul, and until Washington fired The Shot, that bonus free throw was the difference.

This was not a game for the faint of heart. Seeing the seven-foot spectre of Ewing clad in the silver and black, colors so feared by NFL foes of the Los Angeles Raiders, only fortified the aura of Hoya Paranoia in the Dome.

But then, Washington cut all that is Georgetown down to size with his last one-on-one move past Michael Jackson.

"Coach (John Thompson) said in the huddle they'd clear out for Pearl, and they did," said Jackson, Washington's opposite number at the point. "He made a great play. He's a great player."

SU's shot at victory came when freshman Derek Brower—inserted in the closing minutes when center Rony Seikaly joined forward Wendell Alexis on the bench with five personal fouls—deflected a Perry McDonald pass to Andre Hawkins. SU was down one, but now had the ball and 34 seconds remaining to be played.

Following a timeout, Washington drove the right side. "Ewing was there," he said, "and I pulled it out."

After each team called time at the 16-second mark, SU's plan was clear. "It was Dwayne all the way," said SU coach Jim Boeheim, "and hope for the best."

The Orangemen were going to put it up, not wait until the final second.

"We did once, against St. John's, and won (on a Greg Monroe jumper last year)," said Boeheim. "I'm not going to do that again."

When Reggie Williams' inbounds pass sailed out of bounds over David Wingate, SU only had to handle the final four ticks of the clock. Brower collided with Jackson, but a foul was called elsewhere, Horace Broadnax sending Washington to the line for a one-and-one. Brower sweated the call, though.

"He grabbed me or hooked me," he said. "I guess it's an old Georgetown trick. I suppose they did it to me because I was the freshman out there."

One Washington free throw and Jackson's desperation heave that nestled in Raf Addison's arms brought a sea of fans onto the floor, SU, a three-time loser to Georgetown a year ago, including that memorable overtime game in the Big East Tournament, had sprung the upset.

JOHN BERRY, THE SYRACUSE NEWSPAPERS

PEARL WASHINGTON DRIVES FOR THE GAME-WINNING SHOT AGAINST GEORGETOWN IN 1985.

And in so doing, the Hoyas lost consecutive games (Saturday by one to St. John's) for the first time since Ewing was a freshman. It left the Hoyas 7-2 and SU 5-3 in a Big East chase with Villanova (5-2), all pursuing St. John's (7-0).

This was The Shot II. The Shot, the original, was Pearl's midcourt buzzer-beater against Boston College a year ago. But for an Orange team in search of a smooth run through a conference allowing even its finest teams the challenge of battling heavy seas nearly every time out, this was its finest moment, though not its best performance.

ORANGE CROWD OF 32,229 HAS ITS ROTTEN APPLES

32,229 FANS REJOICE IN 65-63 WIN

JANUARY 29, 1985 | BY BOB SNYDER, SYRACUSE HERALD-JOURNAL

John Thompson had yanked his Georgetown University team from the Carrier Dome's playing floor, Jim Boeheim had grabbed the public address microphone.

It wasn't to present a 1,000-point club award to a Syracuse University player.

Monday night, various regions of the country saw the best and worst of Big East basketball. From Pearl Washington's deciding jumper to the smooth shooting of Raphael Addison and the physical power of giant Patrick Ewing, a 65-63 SU victory was worth watching on any evening.

But a crowd of 32,229—the third largest basketball gathering ever under the Dome—had its rotten apples.

Perhaps oranges is more appropriate, because that's what met the back of the backboard early in the game, while Ewing was missing the first free throw of a two-shot foul. Because of the disturbance, he was awarded an extra shot, and ultimately scored two points on his trip to the line.

They cleaned the glass and played on, through the Hoyas' nine-point lead and later, SU's eight-point cushion. At game's end, hundreds and hundreds of fans stormed the court, knocking two radio stations off the air and showing little regard for anyone's safety.

At halftime, Big East commissioner Dave Gavitt, analyst for one of two telecast teams last night, said, "Ironically, we have less trouble in the Dome than anyplace in the conference." After the game, Gavitt merely shook his head in bewilderment.

Boeheim, who said he won't stand for objects being thrown on the court, also declared:

"I don't like the foul line cheer (an obscenity). That's bush. We've got to get rid of it. But overall, our fans are great. They're as well-mannered as anywhere in the country."

"It's not that different (than other Big East arenas)," said Hoya forward David Wingate, following a 2-for-13 shooting game. "It's just that the noise is a little louder."

"It psyches up the opponent," Hoya guard Michael Jackson said of the maddening crowd.

"The Dome is a great place to play, great atmosphere," said Thompson.

"Eastern basketball needs this atmosphere. I don't blame the people here. Some are going to come in here and lose perspective. But we're not talking about a technical foul; somebody can get hurt."

Still, Thompson—who declared "Manley Field House officially closed," after his Hoyas snapped SU's home win streak in the last game played there—supports the Dome and the nation's largest college basketball crowds.

"I'd worry,' he said, "about the Big East if you couldn't get atmospheres like this come tournament time."

FANS STORM THE DOME FLOOR AFTER PEARL AND CO. BEAT GEORGETOWN.

93

Hoyas Intimidate—
and Win Again

MARCH 9, 1987 | BOB SNYDER, SYRACUSE HERALD-JOURNAL

New York—So is the glass Jim Boeheim holds half full or half empty?
After all, his Syracuse basketball team was staying home in the Carrier Dome for the NCAA's party of 64—win or lose against Georgetown, they'd be home. And, oh, how the 26-6 Orange knows all about losing to the Hoyas in Big East Tournament finals.

The Orangemen did it for a third time in as many tries on a balmy Sunday afternoon, 69-59. The reward? A No. 2 seed in the East. Home court. Nasty words about unfair advantage from Nevada-Las Vegas coach Jerry Tarkanian. And a Friday night date with Georgia Southern.

For the first eight minutes of Sunday's eighth annual Big East final, SU looked like a team destined to end the Hoya's unblemished championship record. It was the Pittsburgh game (which SU won, 99-85, Saturday) all over again. The scoreboard read 24-15 with 11:53 remaining before intermission.

Sherman Douglas was playing alley-oop with Rony Seikaly, and Howard Triche was playing swish with the net on jump shots. After shooting 78 percent in the first half the day before against Pitt, the Orange was back at it again, netting nine of its first 10 shots.

Then, the Georgetown defense appeared on stage. The curtain came down on SU. The last 32 minutes, SU shot 31 percent, scored 35 points and made the rapid transformation from brilliance (and as much as a 10-point lead) to bewilderment.

So SU takes its act back home to see if it'll play better far from Manhattan's bright lights. On comes the 20-10 Eagles from Statesboro, Georgia, and the Trans America Conference. Just a few years ago, the conference gave us Houston Baptist's Anicet Lavodrama, most valuable player on the all-name team.

Meanwhile, Sunday's hot weather might better have fit the New York Mets' opener at Shea Stadium than Reggie and the Miracles, the closing act at the Garden.

But Reggie Williams—tournament MVP and superstar of the 26-4 Hoyas, top seed in the Southeast Regional—certainly closed this show with authority. His 25 points against SU gave him a tourney-record 71, one more than Pearl Washington last year and two more than this year's Orange point guard, Sherman Douglas.

"He's everywhere," said SU co-captain Greg Monroe. "We were trying to find where he was on the floor."

"They didn't play me," said Williams. "I thought they'd trap me, but they didn't." That's because the Orange couldn't get their sneakers moving quickly enough to get out on the wing and challenge him.

But Williams' coach did.

"More than anyone we've had at Georgetown, we've had to ask him to use his individual skills," said Thompson. "I called him some names and told him to stop passing and shoot the (bleeping) ball.

"But when I ask him to follow, he follows (which he did when the lead actors were Patrick Ewing, David Wingate and Michael Jackson) . . . . When I ask him to lead, he leads."

SU's offense had shut down for the afternoon. The script was written.

It's a scenario Georgetown has written so often, and not just against Syracuse. It just seems that way.

And it just seems that the Hoyas' bench is two or three rows deep. Actually, Thompson did play 11 guys in the first eight minutes. But there were only five on the floor at the same time.

"You have one man beat, there's another man there," Seikaly said of the Hoyas' defense.

SU's numbers are different.

"We're dependent on the five people we've been going with this year," said Boeheim.

Sunday, some of them didn't show up.

---

game summary | m a r c h 8, 1 9 8 7

SYRACUSE (59)

	m	fg-fga	ft-fta	pf	r	a	pts
Coleman	29	4-7	0-0	4	7	1	8
Triche	38	4-7	2-2	2	2	3	10
Seikaly	36	7-12	5-6	3	8	1	19
Douglas	39	8-19	3-4	4	3	8	20
Monroe	36	1-5	0-0	3	4	5	2
Brower	10	0-3	0-0	0	1	0	0
Thompson	6	0-4	0-0	0	0	0	0
Harried	6	0-1	0-0	0	0	0	0
Team					5		
Totals	200	24-58	10-12	16	30	18	59

GEORGETOWN (69)

	m	fg-fga	ft-fta	pf	r	a	pts
McDonald	37	1-9	4-4	2	8	1	6
Williams	35	9-21	2-3	3	9	1	25
Gillery	1	0-0	0-0	1	0	0	0
Bryant	19	0-2	2-2	3	2	4	2
Tillmon	20	3-6	2-3	0	3	3	8
Highsmith	21	5-9	1-1	3	7	0	11
Winston	22	1-4	0-1	0	2	7	2
Jackson	10	2-2	0-0	1	0	0	6
Smith	12	1-7	0-0	0	2	1	3
Edwards	12	2-2	0-0	1	7	0	4
Jefferson	5	0-0	0-0	0	1	0	0
Allen	6	1-1	0-0	0	1	0	2
Team					5		
Totals	200	25-63	11-14	14	47	17	69

Halftime score: Georgetown 39, Syracuse 32
Officials: Larry Lembo, Tim Higgins, Jim Burr.
Attendance: 19,591
All-Tournament Team: F—Reggie Williams, Georgetown (MVP); F—Jerome Lane, Pittsburgh; C—Rony Seikaly, Syracuse; G—Sherman Douglas, Syracuse; G—Billy Donovan, Providence.

statistics

New Orleans-Bound!

SU's Off to Final Four as NC Falls

MARCH 22, 1987 | BY RICK BONNELL, SYRACUSE HERALD AMERICAN

East Rutherford, N.J.—Jim Boeheim said it best: His Orangemen just wouldn't lose. And because that is so, you had better develop a quick taste for jambalaya and blackened fish. They've made it all the way down the Road to New Orleans.

With their best rebounding performance of the season, a 15-point lead and the iron will of a champion, Syracuse University defeated North Carolina, 79-75, Saturday afternoon in the East Regional final before 19,552 at Byrne Arena.

And now SU meets Big East-rival Providence College—an 88-73 winner over Georgetown in the Southeast Regional final—Saturday at the Louisiana Superdome.

This will be the Orangeman's first trip to the Final Four since 1975, when Boeheim served as an assistant under Roy Danforth.

The top-seeded Tar Heels tested the second-seeded Orangemen thoroughly, shredding SU's lead from the commanding 15 points with 16:09 left, to a narrow three with 2:04 remaining.

Yes, the Orangemen stumbled Saturday, but they never fell. SU point guard Sherman Douglas (14 points) and forward Derrick Coleman (8) both missed the front ends of one-and-ones in the last 1:22. But with 26 seconds left, Coleman pulled in one of his 14 rebounds—this off a Ranzino Smith miss of a driving jumper—and senior Greg Monroe (10 points) followed by hitting two free throws to put the Tar Heels away for good.

"We missed a lot of free throws," said Boeheim—14 in 29 tries, to be exact. "But we never fell backward."

Not only did the Orangemen beat the glamour team of college basketball for the first time since the 1975 Final Four run, but they did so by leading from start to finish.

"We've got a great ballclub," said Douglas. "We can't lose. If it's not me, it's one of the seniors. Each game it's another star."

SU center Rony Seikaly shined as the brightest of all stars, scoring 26 points to be named the East Regional's Most Outstanding Player.

"As soon as we beat Western Kentucky (a week ago today in the Carrier Dome), we knew something special was going on," said Seikaly, who also hauled in 11 rebounds.

He added to that feeling by helping Coleman control UNC's brilliant freshman, J.R. Reid. After scoring 31 points against Notre Dame Thursday, Reid, the 6-foot-9 center/forward, scored just 15 against SU. Further, Reid managed just six rebounds, none of which were grabbed in the first half.

SU started fast, scoring the game's first eight points in less than three minutes. Seikaly registered two of those baskets by following up missed shots, and Coleman did his share, too, rejecting a short jumper by Tar Heel forward Dave Popson.

In all, Seikaly and Coleman had 25 of SU's 42 rebounds, as the Orangemen thumped UNC on the boards by 10. By halftime, SU was ahead by 11 points and had outrebounded the bigger Tar Heels, 29-12. It was the most rebounds by SU in a half this season.

Boeheim stressed after the loss to Georgetown in the Big East Tournament final that his players weren't rebounding the ball well enough to be a great team. SU's previous weakness on the boards became its strength in the NCAAs. In the four-game run to the Final Four—with victories over Georgia Southern, Western Kentucky, Florida and North Carolina—SU has outrebounded each of its foes.

"I thought in the first half, without a doubt, we were at our best rebounding," said Boeheim. "Derrick was so excited today—he

missed a few free throws—but he was up."

Getting the Orangemen up was a job Seikaly assumed. He said he was walking the halls of SU's hotel past midnight Friday, going from room to room to ignite his teammates.

"I never felt," said Seikaly, "so excited, so psyched up, for a game."

UNC scored its first points 3:06 into the game, when Joe Wolf (12 points) came way out

JIM BOEHEIM IS SURROUNDED BY HIS JUBILANT PLAYERS AFTER THEY DEFEATED NORTH CAROLINA TO ADVANCE TO THE FINAL FOUR IN 1987.

front to hit a shot from three-point range. Monroe fouled Wolf on the shot, and Wolf hit the resulting free throw.

UNC put on a run to close the lead to two at 17-15, on a shot by Reid off a Douglas turnover with 13:25 left in the first half.

But that's when the Orangemen put on their bug rush, scoring eight of the next 10 points. Seikaly took over in the lane, with two baskets. Then Boeheim went to his sometimes undependable bench, and the subs came through as well.

Derek Brower, Herman Harried and Stephen Thompson all played fine defense in

SU's 2-3 zone. Thompson, a freshman guard, even grabbed his own miss of a free throw, working inside for a bucket and SU's 41-31 halftime lead.

The surge continued through the initial minutes of the second half, when SU scored 12 of the first 20 points to take its biggest lead of the game. That 15-point margin came on a Howard Triche jumper with 15:43 left.

What looked like a comfortable edge evaporated in just two minutes and 43 seconds of scoreless SU basketball. During that stretch, the Orangemen missed five straight shots as UNC stripped the lead down to four.

"We had to get our composure. We weren't getting the right shots," said Seikaly. "But it was just offensive. Defensively, we were OK."

After Kenny Smith (25 points) hit his three-point jumper to cut SU's lead to three with 2:04 remaining, teammate Jeff Lebo fouled Douglas, putting SU's sophomore point guard in the one-and-one.

Douglas missed but Kenny Smith's three-point reply was long. Reid fouled Coleman in the jostle for the rebound and Coleman also missed his front-end foul shot.

But SU's freshman power forward came through for the victory with the rebound of Ranzino Smith's miss.

"We were underdogs," Douglas said. "But we proved something to everyone."

DERRICK COLEMAN HUGS STEVIE THOMPSON AFTER SYRACUSE'S *79-75* VICTORY OVER THE TAR HEELS.

98

A TITLE SHOT FOR SU

ORANGEMEN DEFUSE PROVIDENCE BOMBS

MARCH 29, 1987 | BY RICK BONNELL, SYRACUSE HERALD AMERICAN

New Orleans—It was supposed to come down to Rony Seikaly's post-up moves vs. Billy Donovan's outside shooting. Or if not that, at least to a question of whether the Orangeman could beat their always-shaky nerves at the free-throw line.

So how do you figure this twist ending? Syracuse University won its biggest game of the Jim Boeheim era Saturday with just the basic skills: rebounding and defense. And because that is so, the Orangemen will play in their first-ever NCAA Tournament championship game, following a 77-63 victory over the Friars before an NCAA-record crowd of 64,959 at the sold-out Superdome.

The Orangemen now face Indiana, a 97-93 winner over Nevada-Las Vegas, in Monday's 8 p.m. title game.

This was not the slam-dunking, push-it-up-the-floor team SU fans think of immediately. This was an SU team that shot below 50 percent from the field (45.3) for the first time in this tournament. But the Orangemen outrebounded the Friars, 53-35, and held Providence to its lowest scoring total in more than two months.

The biggest factor in that defensive effort was shutting down Billy Donovan, previously the NCAA Tournament's top scorer. Donovan scored a season-low eight points, on 3-of-12 shooting.

Only one Providence player, reserve guard Carlton Screen, reached double-figure scoring with 18 points. All five of SU's starters, paced by Greg Monroe's 17 points, scored 10 or more.

"For them to hold this team to 63 points means they're playing great basketball," said Providence coach Rick Pitino. "They definitely have a great chance at the national championship."

They have that chance primarily through the play of freshman power forward Derrick Coleman and sophomore point guard Sherman Douglas. Coleman pulled down 12 rebounds, made two blocks and two steals, and scored 12 points, Douglas scored 12 points, handed out six assists, and squirmed through traffic in the lane for an amazing 11 rebounds.

"When Sherman Douglas, a six-foot point guard, gets 11 rebounds, well, we can beat anybody," said Seikaly, SU's center, who finished the game with 16 points and six rebounds.

99

A massive crowd of Syracuse fans gathers on the streets of the Syracuse campus to celebrate the victory over Providence to advance the Orangemen to the NCAA finals.

Douglas said he saw early in this game that it would not be SU's best offensive performance of the season.

"Really, our offense was all out of sync. It was a sloppy game," said Douglas. "But it was our defense that won it. People think Syracuse plays no defense, because we fast-break so much. They forget we have the best field-goal percentage defense in the big East."

Boeheim said the key to that defense was Douglas, who shadowed Donovan from start to finish. Douglas said Donovan favors going to his right, so Douglas shaded him in that direction and virtually nullified the Friars' best player.

Providence shot only 36 percent from the field, as the Friars missed 10 of their first 12 shots, including nine in a row. Pitino said his team's early shooting problems were due in part to tightness, but SU's man-to-man defense certainly played a role in the Friars falling out of their patterns.

"We played Providence the same way we did the first two times," said Boeheim of two previous victories this season over SU's Big East Conference opponent. "You've got to play man-to-man against them. The key was the defensive end."

"We were just more aggressive on the boards," said Coleman, who helped SU grab eight rebounds off Orange misses at the free-throw line. "I knew rebounding would be a big factor in this game."

100

Sadly, It Slips Away

MARCH 31, 1987 | BY RICK BONNELL, SYRACUSE HERALD-JOURNAL

New Orleans—"Four seconds," Jim Boeheim said with the hint of a sigh, "is an eternity."

At the very least, it would have been a chance. A chance for the winning shot that eluded Boeheim's Orangemen here Monday night, costing Syracuse University its first NCAA championship in basketball.

With just over four seconds left, Indiana University point guard Keith Smart pulled up for a 16-foot jump shot along the left baseline. His shot, launched over the outstretched arms of Howard Triche, licked the rim and fell smoothly through the net for a 74-73 Hoosier lead.

And though each SU player who was on the floor claims he signaled timeout, none was called until a single second remained. Without the time to work a real play, the Orangemen tried a desperation lob pass that was intercepted by Smart to secure the Hoosier victory before 64,959 at the Louisiana Superdome.

It was appropriate that Smart, named Most Outstanding Player, finished the game with the ball in his hands. After all, Smart had scored 12 of the Hoosiers' last 15 points, while the Orangemen concentrated their defense on stopping All-American guard Steve Alford.

But it was the officials, not the foes, who stuck in each Orangeman's mind following the game.

"They should have looked at the monitors," said SU point guard Sherman Douglas, who finished with 20 points. "Considering the importance of this game, they really should have looked at the monitors and reset the clock."

Triche and co-captain Greg Monroe both claim they called timeout with their hands and their voices immediately. But more than two seconds ran off the clock before the game was halted.

"I doubt if you could hear it," Monroe said of his request for a timeout. "But I signaled with my hands."

That SU needed the timeout was the result of a 23-second turnaround that proved to be SU's demise. Smart fouled freshman Derrick Coleman in the backcourt, immediately after Smart closed SU's lead to one point on a drive to the basket with 31 seconds remaining.

Coleman then went to the free-throw line for a one-and-one, and Boeheim pulled his team back off the lane, attempting to set up his defense against a likely three-point try by Alford.

DERRICK COLEMAN SHOOTS INSIDE OVER INDIANA'S DEAN GARNETT.

"First, I want to thank Daryl for not taking the shot, and passing the ball back to me," said Smart, who finished with 21 points. "It was a wise decision."

The Orangemen say they, too, made a wise choice during the sequence, playing a box-and-one, with Douglas shadowing Alford.

"We did our job," said Douglas. "We made someone other than Alford shoot. They just hit a great shot."

That great shot, and the missed free throw that set it up, spoiled an otherwise magnificent performance by Coleman. The freshman's 19 rebounds fell only three short of resetting an NCAA title-game record.

"Coleman rebounded as well as I can remember anybody rebounding the ball," said Boeheim. "We had more than our shot to win the game. But, in those situations you've got to hit your free throws."

The Orangemen had led by as many as eight points in the second half. The largest lead of the game came with 13:09 left, when Triche's 18-foot jump shot gave SU a 52-44 edge.

But in only three minutes and three seconds, Indiana had chopped up SU's lead, going ahead, 54-52, with just under 10 minutes remaining.

That's when Indiana coach Bob Knight, who won his third NCAA title, looked for the Orangemen to fold up for the night.

"I've seen a lot of games where you just keep it going," said Knight. "Where the team that has come from behind eventually is 10 or 12 ahead. Syracuse made a tremendous effort right there to go back on top in the ballgame."

SU's backcourt scored the game's next seven points, as Monroe hit a 17-footer, and Douglas added two free throws and a three-pointer.

Then, the Orangemen got sloppy, and it

But Coleman's first free-throw attempt clanged off the front of the rim, to the right of the mark.

"My hands were sweaty, and as I threw it up, I knew it was off right," said Coleman. "I said, 'Damn! It's off.'"

The Hoosiers worked the clock down to about seven seconds, when the ball went inside to Indiana forward Daryl Thomas. Thomas looked to shoot, saw that SU's box-and-one zone had him well covered, and pushed the ball out to Smart along the baseline.

cost them dearly. On consecutive possessions, SU threw away the ball on bad passes. First, freshman guard Stephen Thompson threw the ball over his shoulder on a drive to the basket, missing Seikaly. Then, Coleman tried a lob pass to Seikaly in the lane that sailed out of Seikaly's reach.

The Hoosiers saw a crack and pushed all the way through, tying the game at 61-61 with 5:38 remaining on a Smart layup.

The Orangemen had spent most of their defensive energy finding various ways to disrupt Alford, who had scored 33 points in a semifinal victory over Nevada-Las Vegas. Boeheim said that if Alford had another 30-plus scoring performance, the Orangemen were finished.

SU started the game in a 2-3 zone, but found it insufficient; someone had to be on Alford's nose at every step. Over the course of the game, four different Orangemen—Triche, Thompson, Monroe and Douglas—each covered Alford, either man-to-man or in the box-and-one.

The strategy did seem to limit Alford's scoring in Indiana's halfcourt offense. The senior shooting guard scored only four points in the game's last 11 minutes.

But in taking away Alford's shot, SU conceded Smart's drives. Twice in the last two minutes, Smart used his speed to push into the lane and tie the game. The second of those drives was set up when Triche missed his second free throw on a one-and-one with 31 seconds left.

Boeheim said pulling his players off the free-throw line that time might have averted

INDIANA'S KEITH SMART HITS THE GAME-WINNING BASKET OVER SU'S HOWARD TRICHE TO WIN THE NCAA CHAMPIONSHIP.

Smart's drive. He wasn't taking any chances the second time, on Coleman's one-and-one.

"I really thought we had an edge the whole last part of the game," said Boeheim.

But the edge fell short, just like Coleman's free throw.

"What can you do?" Douglas pondered. "I'm not going to go out and overdose myself, I'm happy about this season. We know we're going to be contenders next season."

103

HARRY DiORIO, THE SYRACUSE NEWSPAPERS

Dejection shows on the faces of the Syracuse bench (above) while elation is apparent as Indiana University's Keith Smart (right) raises the Final Four trophy after winning the 1987 NCCA finals.

THE SYRACUSE NEWSPAPERS

Syracuse Basketball: A Century of Memories

SU's Program Hits the Top

PAST HEARTACHES, HEROISM BUILT SOLID FOUNDATION

MARCH 31, 1987 | BY BOB SNYDER, SYRACUSE HERALD-JOURNAL

There is no more reason to doubt a program. Or its coach.

Oh, they lost The Game, you say.

Well, where were the Tar Heels and Runnin' Rebels, the Cardinals and Hoyas when all this was going on? This show was primetime, one-on-one against the Academy Awards. Those other teams had discarded their Nikes days or weeks ago, and only Syracuse orange and Indiana red remained for collegiate basketball's colorful last dance.

And one helluva final whirl they gave it in New Orleans. One to be mentioned among the great championships of any time. One for VCRs so Syracusans yet to come can see it and feel as proud as we are.

So look at the Superdome's scoreboard story—IU 74, SU 73—if you choose. And if you see the glass half empty, than surely next season you'll not see it half full either.

Such is the life of the fickle fan.

Then there is the reality of what has happened to a town and its team. Yes, in this love-hate relationship we have with Syracuse University basketball and its mentor, James Arthur Boeheim, we have surely come to accept them as our team and him, our coach.

There is pain today.

Because they did keep score this final game. Because the last shot swished, and Keith Smart played for Indiana. Because precious seconds were lost before total heartache set in.

Without all that, the NCAA need not have waited till last night to hand another trophy to General Robert Montgomery Knight and proclaim Smart most valuable of all tournament players. After Nevada-Las Vegas shot craps from three-point land, they could have hoisted the championship banner in Bloomington.

But, no, there was no submission in the 38th game of an Orange season that was unlike any other. Instead, this was a declaration.

With all it accomplished in winning 31 games, in sending Carolina home early, in making it to the grandest party in all of collegiate sport, Syracuse basketball proclaimed itself at the very top of the game in more than turnstile count.

It takes a Final Four breakthrough. And more.

There had been, after all, SU's kids from a dozen years ago who played their way to San Diego . . . coach Roy Danforth's squad led by Rudy 'n The Rat, centered by Wide-Body Earnie, who spelled his name funny and sometimes traversed the floor in similar fashion.

Athletes never like to hear they over-achieved, but the 1975 bunch did precisely that one glorious evening in the East Regional in Providence. They have never received their just due from their university. They share in this 1987 celebration.

Ditto, Dave Bing. And Mike Lee and Mark Wadach, little guys who played big above the dirt floor at Manley, whose scrappy style of play set a standard for future Orange teams.

There have been so many to bring us to this day. But if we party without toasting The Pearl, then we observe the current SU squad, literally, with tunnel vision. The scope of this program and its recruiting—gained initially through the Big East Conference, Carrier Dome, increased media attention—surely benefited from Dwayne Washington.

It took a different mix, however, to raise the Orange postseason game another level from all those Marches gone sour.

It took a Sherman Douglas pointing the way on both ends of the floor. And rookie Derrick Coleman attacking the boards as if all long rebounds were his. Monday night, they were.

It took our town's Howard Triche and Rochester's Greg Monroe, seniors bent not on the NBA draft but on winning. And the Greek Alp, Rony Seikaly, unleashing an inside arsenal now marvelously developed.

It took enough of a bench (Stevie Thompson, Derek Brower) to make it all possible. Because, you see, the history of NCAA champions is not one of quality minutes turned in by benches running deep.

And it took coach Jim who, says he, is no better coach today than a few weeks ago. Or, he might tell us, no better than before/during/after any of his 261 victories or 84 defeats.

Now, though, he has fought the big war with the General. For those who still doubted, he has held up exceedingly well.

Some folks seem to suggest that he is now undergoing a transformation, and he will turn up for the start of practice on October 15 acting like Dick MacPherson. Rest assured that little Elizabeth Boeheim has done wonders for her daddy, but such a change could only be preceded by something equally cataclysmic—like Bobby Knight embracing the press.

And what's the big deal, anyway? Boeheim is paid to coach, not be a PR man. If he hadn't provided 261 reasons why he can coach, than a 262nd Monday night in Louisiana would not change that.

What has changed, however, is a feeling one senses.

In 1959, when Ben Schwartzwalder's team won a championship, it wasn't the same. There's no Final Four on the gridiron. And the university's fear of a football factory pointed the program in the wrong direction, which is where it headed not so many years later.

A dozen years ago, with that first trip to the Final Four, we witnessed a dream come true for the moment. But a basketball program was not yet ready to step forward and declare itself among the elite.

Today, we are ready to do that. With Seikaly and Coleman inside, Douglas, Thompson and academic redshirt Earl Duncan outside, there is reason to think Final Four '88.

When you've covered so many March dreams dashed—17 postseason tournaments, the previous 16 in succession—you share with thousands of others in your town a wish to have been in New Orleans. Not just to dine at Antoine's.

To taste the moment with a basketball

program that has played its way, through both growing pains and lucky bounces, all the way to the top.

Reason for me to already reserve a week in '88.

Goin' to Kansas City, Kansas City, here I come!

But first, a town that has been wearing orange on its heart for days now, is ready to show just how big-time it is. The collegiate basketball world knows this was no one-shot deal.

So c'mon, Syracuse. Dry those tears, there's reason to celebrate!

STEVE PARKER, SU ACO

SYRACUSE'S 1987 FINAL FOUR TEAM.

The Final Two Minutes of the 1987 Title Game Between SU and Indiana

2:03 SU leads 70-68. Rony Seikaly hits layup, is fouled, misses free throw: Derrick Coleman rebounds, Sherman Douglas misses driving flip shot.

1:21 Indiana's Keith Smart hits reverse layup. 70-70.

0:57 Howard Triche makes 7-foot jump shot in the lane, SU 72-20.

0:39 Smart miss shot, Triche rebounds, is fouled by Steve Alford.

0:38 Indiana timeout.

0:38 Triche makes first, misses second, SU 73-70.

0:32 Smart makes eight-foot shot in the lane SU 73-72.

0:30 Indiana timeout.

0:28 Coleman is fouled.

0:28 Indiana timeout.

0:28 Coleman misses first of one-and-one.

0:04 Smart makes 16-foot jumper from left side. IU 74-73.

0:01 SU timeout: Indiana timeout. Smart intercepts Coleman's inbound pass. Game over.

|timeline|

ALLEY-OOP

DOUGLAS CATALYST FOR SIX OF THEM AGAINST FRIARS

JANUARY 29, 1989 | BY DONNA DITOTA, SYRACUSE HERALD AMERICAN

The moment spans only seconds. Its aftermath leaves participants pumping their fists and crowds roused into a cheering frenzy.

The Syracuse University Orangemen showcased the alley-oop play before 32,096 Carrier Dome fans Saturday in SU's 100-96 win over Providence.

Six times, SU point guard Sherman Douglas lofted a pass toward the basket that one of his teammates caught and slammed through the rim.

Six times, the Carrier Dome crowd rose in unison to roar with delight.

It is one of college basketball's most explosive offensive weapons, a play that ignites both quarterback and receiver. It is a play the Orangemen have mastered under Douglas' direction.

The six-foot point guard collected 22 assists Saturday to tie an NCAA mark for assists in a single game, break a Big East mark, and set a new SU single-game assist record.

Douglas racked up the numbers on a variety of passes, but it is the alley-oop pass that perhaps has earned him the reputation as one of college basketball's craftiest passers.

Douglas said he and his teammates don't practice the play much. It's more instinctive, he says, more feel.

Douglas spies a teammate inside or on the wing, makes eye contact and delivers. The onus then shifts to the receiver, who must catch the pass, then complete the slam.

"He throws it as soon as you make eye contact," said SU forward David Johnson, who combined with Douglas for one alley-oop basket Saturday. "He wants to put the ball on the corner of the basket for you, right on an angle."

Douglas and Johnson say the play works particularly well against zone defenses, when opponents aren't responsible for checking a single man. Douglas shades to a side, then spots a teammate creeping toward the basket on the weak side. Seconds later, the ball becomes airborne.

"The defender, most of the time, isn't aware of who's behind him," Johnson said. "(The defense) is focusing in one direction, and Sherm just puts the ball up there."

"And once the ball gets up in the air and (defender) is looking at it, it's all over," Douglas said.

SU's execution of the alley-oop shouldn't come as any surprise to opposing teams. Opponents study reels of film on the Orangemen and can almost spy Douglas-to-Stevie Thompson connections in their sleep.

But knowing about SU's affection for the alley-oop play and knowing how to defend it can be two different things.

"We knew they were going to do it, but we haven't seen a team like that before," Providence forward Marty Conlon said. "You turn your head and that quickly, they run the alley-oop."

Providence coach Rick Barnes was asked to comment on his team's failure to react better to the play. During one stretch in the first half, the Orangemen scored six points in just over two minutes off alley-oop passes.

Barnes offered this simple explanation:

"Number one, they have a guy who throws an exceptional pass, and number two, they have some athletes who can go up and get it," he said.

109

SYRACUSE UNIVERSITY GUARD SHERMAN DOUGLAS SHOWCASES A LAYUP IN THE 1987 BIG EAST CONFERENCE GAME AGAINST PITTSBURGH. DOUGLAS SCORED A TOURNAMENT RECORD OF 35 POINTS.

Orangemen Celebrate After Victory, but the War's Not Over Yet

MARCH 5, 1990 | BY BUD POLIQUIN, SYRACUSE HERALD-JOURNAL

After it was over, after the Orangemen had survived this most recent exposure to the Georgetown beast Sunday afternoon, the lampshade very nearly became the headdress of choice inside the Syracuse locker room.

The SU guys, so giddy that they actually stopped to converse with the dolts from the media, had won both a game and a regular-season conference championship before a record, and raving, house of 33,015.

And now it was time to have their backs slapped by such visiting clubhouse luminaries as Ernie Banks, Spike Lee, Louis Orr and Dick MacPherson—none of whom, by the way, had been able to clear his schedule to take in the Lafayette tilt earlier in the season.

"The fans would have had to go home and cry," submitted Jim Boeheim, the curator of Syracuse basketball. "Now, they can go out and have a good time. I'm sure all the restaurants are happy, too."

Get the idea here? If laughs had been snowflakes, a plow would have been needed to rescue the Orangemen from the Carrier Dome in the aftermath of their 89-87 overtime conquest of seventh-ranked Georgetown.

But while Sunday's chortling was hardly out of line, perhaps a more appropriate response to their good deed might have been for the SU fellows, as well as their fans, to heave a sigh of relief.

Indeed, the Orangemen may have completed an historic home-and-home sweep of the Hoyas, a fact that was afterward saluted on the court by Billy Owens and his bold brushing motion. But then, not before the folks from Washington had provided the broom.

Accordingly, what follows is the list of gifts presented to Boeheim and his gang:

• A 10-point play, inspired by three technical fouls (by three different officials) on Georgetown coach John Thompson, that turned an Orange deficit of 36-33 into an Orange lead of 43-36 two minutes removed from the intermission.

• The subsequent banishment of Thompson, the 6-foot-10, 300-pound sage who was forced to sit out the game's final 27:14 somewhere in the catacombs of the building.

SU's Billy Owens drains two free-throws to send the game against Georgetown into overtime.

• A foolhardy foul by Sam Jefferson off Owens—who was some 50 feet from the basket at that point—with one second remaining in regulation and the Hoyas ahead, 81-79. Cool Billy, naturally, drained both attempts to send the affair into the extra session.

• A one-rebound, no-block performance out of heretofore sensation Alonzo Mourning, who had a chance to send the game into a second overtime . . . but, in keeping with his afternoon's bleak performance, airballed from 12 feet or so at the buzzer.

• Despite all of that, however—and don't forget to mix in a howling mob and the homecourt advantage—the Orangemen were able to win by a mere basket. In overtime, yet.

So, what was with all the yuks?

"The key is to win the game," explained Michael Edwards, SU's spunky freshman who finished with 18 points. "Whoever has the most amount of points when it's over is what

counts, no matter what else happens. People are going to say we won the game. And that's all that really matters."

Well, yes and no.

Yes, because the records will show forevermore that the No. 10 Orangemen (22-5) won their fourth Big East Conference regular-season title . . . no, because Sunday's emotional triumph, aided as it was, shouldn't exactly be viewed as a reason to just yet book a hotel room in Denver now that the NCAA Tournament is but 10 days away.

"Thompson helped us out because we were down by five or six points," said a rather candid Owens of the spectacular tantrum thrown by the Hoyas' head bear-with-a-towel. "And it's hard to come back on Georgetown. If we had lost this game, I probably wouldn't be talking to anybody right now. It really would have been crazy. A psychological thing."

And to think that "psychological thing"

111

would almost certainly have enveloped our town had Jefferson only possessed enough presence of mind to keep his mitts off of Billy out there near midcourt. A chilling thought, that.

Alas, such is not the case. And so, as the Orangemen head off this weekend to the big city and its garbage heaps for those annual fund-raising exhibition games known as the Big East tournament, the glass is half-filled. Which means McNichols Arena, where this year's Final Four will take to the floor, remains in sight.

"Now, we can think of doing all this stuff again in New York," Boeheim said Sunday. "Georgetown played great because we played great the whole way. I thought we played as well as we could play."

There was some truth in the coach's statement, especially in the performances of Derrick Coleman, Owens and Edwards, who combined for 68 points, 19 rebounds, 15 assists, five steals and four blocks. How much truth, though, as they say, remains to be seen.

But of this, the Orangemen can be dead-solid certain: They should not expect any more of the kinds of special assistance they received Sunday.

"I let my competitive juices overflow," confessed Thompson of his blue-worded raging over a foul call against his club that cost the Hoyas a game. "I made a mistake and that's it. It won't happen again, I don't think.

"I've never gone three-on-one with the officials before. I felt like one of those bowling balls. I jumped in three different ways. I couldn't even get back off the floor."

And then, John—like the Orangemen just down the hall a ways—had to laugh.

You know, it's funny. When Syracuse knocked off the Hoyas in Landover back in January, there were newspaper reports that had Thompson saying something along the lines of, "Wait 'til the next game," to SU fans as he departed.

Sunday, however, there wasn't any such conversation as he strode off. No, the big man merely raised his hands to the masses, and then kind of flapped them to thus inspire a kind of noise usually heard only during air raids.

And afterward, he spoke once more.

"I never said that," Thompson claimed of any ominous warning submitted down at the Capital Centre. "I'm too intelligent to say that. You give the opponent an incentive."

And then, following the slightest of pauses, there was this: "I will say, 'I'll see you in New York,' though."

The Orangemen, too busy celebrating in their locker room, didn't hear. Which was just as well. Why spoil the party?

112

NICHOLAS LISI, THE SYRACUSE NEWSPAPERS

SYRACUSE BASKETBALL COACH JIM BOEHEIM REACTS TO HIS TEAM'S
OVERTIME WIN OVER GEORGETOWN, 89-87, AT THE CARRIER DOME.

More Than Rules
Have Been Violated Here

A PAINFUL TIME FOR ORANGE

OCTOBER 2, 1992 | BY SEAN KIRST, THE POST-STANDARD

Roy Simmons Jr. learned Thursday that the grants-in-aid at the heart of Syracuse University lacrosse were being amputated by the NCAA because of bean-counting errors by SU auditors.

So Simmons was fuming when he faced a room filled with reporters, drawn like moths to the glare of the SU men's basketball program.

"I wonder," Simmons asked, "if we had a press conference today to talk about the problems in Somalia, if you'd all be here."

We know the answer. Simmons, as coach of a "secondary" program, understands that big-time sports in our town, and across the country, often create a frenzied allegiance.

That is enough to draw 33,000 people to a domed stadium on a bitter winter night to watch teenagers play basketball. It generates the money and fanfare to create work for sportswriters, and it causes well-heeled adults to bask in the company of naive young athletes.

Anguish in Somalia? That attracts a sliver of the attention, because a jump shot can offer a screen from real life. But there is a danger, when the lines start to blur, of what the NCAA labeled Thursday as a "serious breakdown."

The ruling resulted in a series of sanctions, which quickly revived the community turmoil that for a time was dormant as the probe dragged on. Fans again will debate the justice of the newly imposed recruiting penalties, of the year away from the almighty tournament of the NCAA.

But what could easily be missed, and what the NCAA barely addressed, is how real people were hurt by a program teetering on the edge.

Indeed, there are many of us who couldn't care less about the penalties, who feel no satisfaction in seeing SU humiliated, but who simply wish for a sign of real worry and change from any of those who speak for the school.

That would be more important than sanctions, which won't set any real example for the decent and engaging kids who make up the SU basketball team—at least not while the penalties are rationalized as persecution.

A couple of months ago, head coach Jim Boeheim explained that he knew nothing of the most notorious violation—the Christmas cards received by players in the locker room in

MIKE HOPKINS, CURRENTLY AN ASSISTANT COACH, PLAYED FOR SYRACUSE FROM 1989-93.

the late 1980s, cards that SU ruled often contained $50 bills.

The veteran SU coach compared it to longtime embezzlement in a firm operated by old friends, where one secretly milks the other. If the payments happened, Boeheim said, they happened without his knowledge, and his players never clued in their coach. That in itself seems sad and unfortunate, a triangle of long-term silence with damaging results.

No one spoke at the news conference about the human debris created by the "breakdown," such as a young woman named Carolyn Ossen. She was an 18-year old SU freshman in 1990, on campus for only three weeks, when security guards found her screaming in a hotel room. She was struggling with highly sought basketball prospect Wilfred Kirkaldy, who was at SU on a recruiting visit.

Ossen would later speak of the dark side of college sports, of an environment in which she watched "groupies" write academic papers for some college athletes. You would think the cult of celebrity that creates such an environment and the room for potential tragedy is more dangerous and demanding of a reaction than meat loaf provided by some starry-eyed booster.

But that's not the NCAA's bailiwick. For instance, there was no mention Thursday of a Syracuse woman whose 14-year-old daughter, just out of eighth grade, became involved in 1989 with an SU basketball player. He later would tell police he was living in the neighborhood, at the home of booster Joseph Giannuzzi, a friend of the girl's family. The woman, whose name has been withheld by *The Post-Standard*, felt her child was too young to handle a sexual relationship.

In a normal situation, such incidents might trigger questions about the moral compass of a program growing too quickly.

115

JIM BOEHEIM FACES SOME TOUGH QUESTIONS AT A PRESS CONFERENCE REGARDING NCAA RULES VIOLATIONS.

But wounded families don't violate NCAA rules. Both cases basically were written off by internal investigators, who never even spoke to Ossen.

Certainly, as Simmons implies, it is fair to say there is a measure of blame for all of us—the media that glorify impressionable kids, or the boosters who endear themselves to home-sick teenagers.

Still, SU makes a business of filling the Carrier Dome, and with the cheering crowds comes a heavier burden. You hope that beyond anger at the media, or denial over the cause of the sanctions, some SU administrators and coaches will realize how their "breakdown" scarred some everyday people.

Editor's Note: Syracuse backed off its recruitment of Kirkaldy.)

116

VIEWPOINTS

Here's what some are saying about the results of the NCAA investigation:

"The way to summarize it best is it's relief, baby, relief. It's got to be a very relieved moment for Jim Boeheim and his staff. They've been operating under such stress and pressure the last couple of years. Let's get on with it, that's got to be the philosophy. I certainly think they can sustain their program at the highest level. I think their program is bigger than this."

—ABC and ESPN analyst Dick Vitale

"Well, they had to penalize us, didn't they? We broke the rules. Although I think the rules are obsolete, antiquated. Someone wants to treat a kid to a sandwich, what's the big deal? It's all hurt business, I suppose, no tournament. But I think the enthusiasm of the fans will continue as long as we have a winning team."

—Varsity restaurant owner Ted Dellas

"I don't think they (the NCAA) really found anything that's worth serious allegations. This is kind of like a slap on the wrist. That it was extended and took so long, that's punishment in itself. You have every coach using it against them in recruiting."

—Ex-SU basketball star Leo Rautins

"I'm quite angry at your newspaper for hurting the university. You've not only done damage to the sports program—and the revenue those sports generate for academic programs—but the community at large. It hurts everybody. Especially now, when recruiting good students is so difficult. Was it worth it?"

—Michael Sickler, president, SU chapter of the American Association of University Professors

"I'm very happy they're continuing to appear on television. I have a great deal of respect for Jim Boeheim and his coaching. His teams are fun to watch. If you take television away, you take away a great recruiting ploy."

—ESPN analyst Larry Conley

117

JIM BOEHEIM SPEAKS TO THE MEDIA.

"Well, it's over with. I think it's been resolved and now we have to move forward. Obviously, you wish it never happened in the first place. But it did. There were penalties and we have to live with them. I'm very comfortable with the way the university reacted and the compliance measures we took to make sure nothing like this happens again."

    —H. Douglas Barclay, chairman, SU's Board of Trustees

"I knew we would get some kind of sanctions, but it was a shock to learn other teams are affected. One of the most important things on campus is SU sports. It's a big part of life here. I'm just glad football's untouched."

    —SU student government President Nick Graciano

"At this time of difficulty for the university, we stand with Chancellor Kenneth Shaw in his determination to see that Syracuse athletic programs move forward. The rule violations have ended and the university has taken steps to make sure they do not occur again."

    —Gov. Mario Cuomo, in statement from his office

SU Zone Defense Razes Arizona

DECEMBER 24, 1995 | BY DONNA DITOTA, SYRACUSE HERALD AMERICAN

Tucson, Ariz.—More than two minutes remained in Saturday's game inside McKale Center, but already, John Wallace and Otis Hill felt confident enough to celebrate.

They bumped chests about 20 feet in front of the Arizona bench, where Wildcats sat dejected and defeated. Hill yelled to the stunned Arizona crowd, which streamed toward the exits with its team trailing by 16 and Lazarus Sims on the free throw line for SU.

"That's right, leave," Hill shouted. "That's right."

They left with an unfamiliar feeling. Their Wildcats had lost.

They Syracuse Orangemen came into the McKale Center, a place where Arizona had compiled a 123-6 record since 1987-88, and beat the nation's third-ranked team, 79-70.

The Orangemen never trailed after the opening of the second half. They shot 50 percent, controlled the tempo and held the Wildcats, a team averaging 86 points a game, to 70.

And they did so while an inferno of red shirts screamed and hollered for the home team.

"It's a very, very big win," said Wallace, who was big himself Saturday with 26 points and nine rebounds. "It's got to rank up there in the top five wins of all time since I've been at this school. Especially being on the road and being one of the few teams to beat them non-conference the last couple of years here."

SU knocked Arizona from the unbeaten ranks with the defense Saturday. The Orangemen started the game in a 2-3 zone and never came out of it. Wildcats point guard Reggie Geary said his team never found its rhythm.

Arizona shot just 39 percent, its worst shooting performance of the season. The Wildcats had been making 54 percent of their shots before SU threw its zone at them.

Syracuse coach Jim Boeheim said he started with a zone as an experiment of sorts. He was "50-50" he said, about whether to start man-to-man or zone. Zone won the coin toss.

Wallace led all scorers with 26. Hill and J.B. Reafsnyder split 22 points. Todd Burgan scored 11, but was just 2-of-12 from the floor.

Sims, facing full-court pressure for most of the second half, accumulated 10 assists against just four turnovers.

119

JOHN WALLACE SHOOTS OVER KENTUCKY'S ANTOINE WALKER IN THE 1996 NCAAs.

120

ORANGE SQUEEZED BY PRESS

JANUARY 1, 1996 | BY DONNA DITOTA, SYRACUSE HERALD-JOURNAL

Honolulu—The game with Syracuse was just minutes old last week when Lute Olson mused about the fate of the Orangemen for the rest of the season.

SU had dominated his Wildcats in Arizona, and Olson credited SU with out-playing his squad. He called SU a good basketball team. And then he wondered about what would happen if the Orangemen ran into a team that could really pressure the basketball.

Plenty of people found out Saturday night.

The Orangemen lost their first game of the season here in the Rainbow Classic, falling to top-ranked University of Massachusetts, 65-47, in the tournament's championship game, SU shot 38 percent in the game. The 47 points were the fewest an Orange team has scored in the Jim Boeheim era. But the telling statistic Saturday, the one that explained the story of this game, occurred in the turnover category. SU committed a season-high 24 turnovers. The Orangemen experienced firsthand the defensive juggernaut UMass represents. And they had to do it for four crucial minutes of the second half, when the Minutemen cracked open a close game with their press.

The Orangemen led, 25-24, and owned possession of the basketball to start the second half. Four minutes later, they trailed by 10.

It was that sudden and that decisive.

"The start of the second half," said SU coach Jim Boeheim, "was the key to the whole basketball game."

"I think it was the turning point of the game," UMass guard Carmelo Travieso said. "We knew we had to step up defensively coming out of the half. We knew we had to make something happen. Our pressure really got to them in that little stretch there and we made the easy plays and really picked it up."

121

UConn's Ray Gun Regains the Touch

MARCH 9, 1996 | BY SEAN KIRST, THE POST STANDARD

New York—Madison Square Garden was quiet Friday, more than an hour to go before Syracuse and Connecticut tipped off, when Ray Allen casually jogged onto the court.

The 6-foot-5, 200-pound swingman wore a plain white T-shirt above his sweatpants, and he stopped to chat a little with Lazarus Sims and John Wallace, who were also shooting around. But Allen had some business to attend to. On Thursday, against Seton Hall, he had shot 4-of-17. He wanted to isolate what had gone wrong.

So he toed up to the foul line and shot 15 free throws in front of 19,000 empty seats, mentally doing a tune-up on his form. Then he backpedaled a few steps to the three-point arc, and did the same thing. He took 15 set shots, his toes never leaving the floor, and only a few of the shots went through the rim.

But it was enough. He had his answer. It had been his legs, he realized. His legs were out of sync when he went up for his jumper. He walked into the locker room, diagnosis complete, and then used the Orangemen to test his theory.

He scored 29 points, 19 in the first half. He shot 11-of-21 from the floor, 4-of-9 from three-point range. Early in the second half, when the Orangemen dropped into a box-and-one to shut off Allen, the rest of the Huskies went nuts. Travis Knight spoke of how the middle seemed to open wide, and 15-foot jumpers became easy.

Stop Allen, and Connecticut still comes at you in waves. The Orangemen wore down despite a terrific effort, and UConn had an 85-67 win and a rematch with Georgetown.

Then Allen sat in an empty locker room, while his own teammates clucked their tongues in disbelief, and insisted he wasn't pleased with his effort. "Not really," said Allen, who won't reveal if he will leave this year for the NBA. "There were somethings I didn't do."

The game isn't all about *scoring*, he said, in the voice of an accountant who's found small problems with his books. There had been a couple of times on defense when he was beaten back door. He would need to remember to do something about that. And there had been that reverse layup he came down and missed. Inexcusable. His next pregame diagnosis might need to deal with *that*.

He failed to mention how the layup was attempted in a sea of Orangemen, all of them leaping and waving their arms. But Allen still argued he wasn't happy with his game. "A triple-double," he said. "When I get one of those, I guess I'm satisfied."

At the Heart of Heroics: A Solemn Bond

WALLACE HITS GAME WINNER AGAINST GEORGIA IN OT

MARCH 23, 1996 | SEAN KIRST, THE POST-STANDARD

Denver—They sat across from each other in the locker room, almost knee to knee, until a crowd of reporters swept in to divide them. "As close as brothers," Lazarus Sims said of John Wallace. On Friday night, amid their triumph, they both recalled their promise to each other.

Four years ago, Sims came down from the bleachers at a court in Glens Falls, where Wallace's Greece-Athena High School team lost in the state Federation championships, and the two of them clasped hands. They promised to stay with each other the whole way through at Syracuse. Last summer, they came within a breath of getting out.

But they stayed, so credit this heroic SU finish to the promise. Wallace played 18 great minutes to finish off Georgia, but he said it could not have happened without Sims. "I knew he would get me the ball," Wallace said. Sims pulled up to sink two three-point jumpers down the stretch, when everyone in the place thought the game was over, when the Bulldogs had built up a nine-point lead.

Now Syracuse University, whose twin senior pistons are Wallace and Sims, is in the Elite Eight for the first time in seven years.

SU won in overtime Friday, 83-81, in a game that seemed over four or five different times. Wallace sat the bench in foul trouble for 10 minutes, blaming himself and a "dumb foul" for SU's collapse. When he finally got back onto the court, his team down by 10 and the Bulldogs on fire, he pulled the other Orangemen in around him.

"We can still win this," he said. "Just get me the ball."

Which is what Sims does better than anybody else.

With 30 seconds left, Wallace took a pass from Sims and dropped in a layup to tie it. Pertha Robinson answered with a jumper for the Bulldogs. With two seconds left, SU took the ball out at midcourt, Wallace handling the inbounds pass, when he looked downcourt and caught Jason Cipolla's eye.

Wallace rifled it overhand, faking Georgia's Shandon Anderson out of the play, and Cipolla dropped in the shot to create overtime. The Orangemen went nuts and swarmed together on the bench, where Wallace told them to calm down, to remember what had

SU's John Wallace shoots the game winner against Georgia in the 1996 NCAAs.

STEPHEN D. CANNERELLI, THE SYRACUSE NEWSPAPERS

happened in the last two NCAA Tournaments. Against Arkansas and Missouri, SU had staged frantic comebacks to collapse in OT, and Wallace said the celebrating had to wait at least five minutes.

"It was the same situation as the last two years," he said.

Then Wallace came out and put his team on his back. He sank two foul shots with 2:06 left that tied it up. He sank a jumper from the foul line to tie it again. On the next SU possession, again down by two, Sims tucked the ball on his hip out on the wing and simply waited for Wallace to fight open underneath.

"Intuition" is how Sims describes their mental bond, which goes back to when they both were in junior high. He fired up a lob just beyond the rim. Wallace went hard and got it, laid it off the glass, and it seemed like maybe Georgia would break down. But Robinson drained a difficult three from the corner. Bedlam, all the old Orange ghosts flying around the court, SU on the brink of going down in OT.

So Wallace took the inbounds pass, turned upcourt, and sprinted toward the hoop. SU coach Jim Boeheim just let Wallace go. He did not call a timeout. This was Wallace's moment, his turn, his shot.

He stopped outside the circle with two seconds left. He sank the three.

Just like that, the ghosts were gone. Wallace had 30 points and 15 rebounds, and Sims had 10 assists. In the locker room, they wanted to speak mainly of each other. They met in eighth grade at an AAU tournament in Rochester, where Wallace marveled at the tricks this Syracuse kid did with the ball.

They stuck together through the birth of Wallace's son, through Sims' long tenure on the SU bench, through Wallace's near-decision to leave for the NBA. Wallace wasn't heartbroken when Michael Lloyd quit school because it guaranteed Sims would run the team.

To Sims, Lloyd had failed to get the ball inside enough to Wallace, and he couldn't imagine watching Wallace call in vain for another year. And Sims was ready to quit the team when his father died last summer, but he in turn knew that Wallace was coming back.

Which is why this golden ending even happened. In the locker room, as the crowd drained away, Wallace stayed behind and kept speaking of Sims, how he couldn't have done any of this without his friend. Sims put his hand on his face and choked up, thankful the promise was extended once again.

SU's JOHN WALLACE HITS THE GAME WINNER IN OVERTIME AGAINST GEORGIA AT THE NCAA's IN DENVER.

125

ONE GAME AWAY

BOEHEIM BASHERS PAY HEED

MARCH 24, 1996 | BY BOB SNYDER, SYRACUSE HERALD AMERICAN

There is no victory for Jim Boeheim.

Winning is losing.

And losing is losing.

That's the essence of a man who, for 20 years, has been the guy winning 24 basketball games a season at Syracuse because he's got all that talent on the Hill and plays non-conference creampuffs.

That view, as seen through the tunnel vision of his critics.

And they are legion.

They're still wondering—notwithstanding John Wallace's 19-foot rope that found nothing but twine and a two-point win over Georgia in the best game of these NCAAs—why didn't Boeheim call a timeout?

Honest, they still think he blew it and 'Cuse won in spite of him.

They've won 27 in spite of him.

Any coach worth a damn, they'll exclaim, calls a TO, baby! You're down to one possession for a shot at the regional championship and you just stand there like a robot in a daze, while some 6-8 kid dribbles and fires from 19 feet away?

If he had called a timeout at the end of OT, and the Orange lost, it would have been Boeheim's fault.

Of course. We understand: the guy can't coach.

By the way, Boeheim bashers, didn't Syracuse's bony, balding, blah, whining coach call a timeout in the dying second of regulation? And didn't SU rescue overtime from the jaws of defeat, and later claim a victory in the most memorable game of these NCAAs?

Just lucky, I guess, huh?

Even now, even after his team is the only unranked preseason team to make it to the Elite Eight and today makes the last stand, as a 6-point underdog, for a Big East in which—clearly—Connecticut, Georgetown and Villanova were better teams.

And still they gather; here, there, everywhere. They call radio talk shows to tell Central New Yorkers, the basketball world, that the record does not speak for itself.

Who says Jim Boeheim's a good coach?

He loses to Richmond, remember? I mean, other than 481 games, what's he won?

The guy had one shot at the big enchilada and look what his kids—yes, more talented than Indiana—did in the closing seconds.

Choked, I suppose.

Right. No discipline, no timeout called 'til precious seconds ran off the clock. Yup. But it seems that Boeheim was every bit the equal of the bombastic bag of wind from Bloomington—albeit one of the best game coaches around—Robert Montgomery Knight.

Get Smart, pal. No pun intended. Indiana won. Boeheim blew it.

And so forever, until James Arthur Boeheim, age 51, walks away from the Orange bench a final time—whatever year, decade, millennium that is—he remains to many a guy lucky to pull down a half-million bucks a year for rolling the ball out at his alma mater.

X's and O's? Discipline? Get real!

Come down, look for Wallace. Shoot the trey. Play the zone. Press if you're desperate. That's Boeheim, circa 1995-96. Right?

Real tough to coach against that guy, huh? Tubby Smith should have beaten him.

Geez, if Tubby's a better coach, why isn't he getting ready for the pregame meal before taking on those favored/taller/deeper/more talented Kansas Jayhawks?

Boeheim lives with so many criticizing him, so few giving him his due. He says it doesn't matter.

Someday, he'll say the Hall of Fame doesn't matter.

It matters, it all matters, because Boeheim—whether you find him personable or lacking in any personality—has mellowed in middle age, while retaining a cutting edge that

JIM BOEHEIM KIDS WITH COACHING PALS P.J. CARLESIMO (LEFT) AND MIKE KRZYZEWSKI (CENTER) AT A 1991 KIDNEY FOUNDATION DINNER.

has never taken kindly to criticism of his coaching.

It's been said during this season, by me and others, that Boeheim has done one of his finest coaching jobs. That's been said in other years about him when, with lesser talent, he's won big.

Control superstars? C'mon, they run all over him, do what they want. Look at Derrick Coleman!

As if Coleman, who marched to his own drummer then as now, has been on any NBA coach's leash.

And Rony Seikaly? Once spoiled, always spoiled.

Close to his players, no. Close to others; not but a few.

So what? We're not inviting James Arthur Boeheim into our home—as if he'd make an ass of himself. We're inviting ourselves into the arena, physically or via our TV screen bringing his team into our hearts.

And for 20 years, Jimmy Boeheim has delivered. Win or lose today, that ain't gonna change, brother.

127

SU Still Dancing

LONG-SHOT ORANGEMEN SHOCK KANSAS

MARCH 25, 1996 | BY SEAN KIRST, THE POST-STANDARD

Denver—The NCAA officials pulled out the yellow step ladder Sunday and put it beneath the basket at the McNichols Sports Arena. Then the Syracuse University Orangemen, all of them, mounted it to cut down the net, strand by strand.

First came Donovan McNabb, star quarterback on the football team, who on this basketball squad has been comic king of stress relief. The rest of the team followed. Elvir Ovcina, who came to the team from troubled Bosnia. David Patrick, the Australian point guard. Marius Janulis, the crewcut Lithuanian who makes up the third leg of Planet Boeheim.

The Orangemen had just beaten Kansas, 60-57, to win a trip to the Final Four. This was the 28th victory for the team that didn't make the preseason Top 25. This was the Syracuse team judged last fall as the weakest in a decade. In a town that survives winter with a Final Four dream, this was a great bunch of kids who started the season with no chance.

To everyone except them.

They mounted the ladder, some laughing, some juking to a rap tune they sang among themselves, something about how "the Cuse is in the house." Up went J.B. Reafsnyder, the awkward freshman who turned himself into a solid senior center. Up went Bernie Fine, Wayne Morgan and Mike Hopkins, the assistant coaches, with their Final Four caps pushed on backward.

Up went Otis Hill, the brawny center whose consistent play carried the day, his weary face lit up in joy. Up went Jim Hayes, reserve commandant of the eccentric Bench Krew, which believes its sidelines antics have helped create all the good luck.

Up went Bobby Lazor, whose difficult season on the bench at least will end in something big. Up went Elimu Nelson, the former walk-on whose dreadlocks bounced as he climbed the yellow steps. No one was forgotten as the net began to fall, strand by strand.

A crowd of Orange cheerleaders and fans stood behind the hoop, and they went nuts for Jason Cipolla, the tough kid from Queens who spent much of the season earning back his starting job. With 12 seconds left, he made the biggest foul shot of his life. A year and a half ago he was playing junior college ball in front of hundreds of people. On Sunday, before an arena filled with screaming Kansas fans, he helped SU make history.

"This team is tight," he said. "We're really all together." The words were echoed by Don Lowe, the trainer who anchors one end of the bench. "No jealousies," Lowe said. "They like each other. This is just a special bunch of kids."

The fans roared for Todd Burgan, who before the game stood on the court sinking foul shot after foul shot, who grabbed big rebounds but missed the free throws that could have made him Sunday's goat. Instead, his teammates hugged him and pushed him toward the ladder, and he went up the steps to bring down what he earned.

Finally, John Wallace and Lazarus Sims climbed the steps together, two seniors locked this season by friendship and by faith. They stood on the top, and Sims held up four fingers, although SU coach Jim Boeheim chose not to make the climb.

"Too tired," he joked later.

More likely he refused because of something else he said, the idea of leaving the spotlight to his players.

Yet, it was Boeheim who huddled his team on the bench three times in the final minutes, with SU clinging to a lead, and mapped out inbounds plays that saved the game. The Orangemen aren't deep in ball-handling skills, but Wallace threw two perfect bombs to Burgan and Cipolla, and dropped another soft pass to Hill.

Who stepped to the line and knocked down both foul shots.

It was Boeheim who turned one of the slowest teams he's ever had into a zone-playing nuisance. And it was Boeheim who walked into the locker room Sunday sweet with this moment, only a year after the sorrow of an

129

SU'S TODD BURGAN CATCHES AN ALLEY-OOP PASS AGAINST KANSAS.

OT loss to Arkansas, and fixed his gaze on the chuckling McNabb. "Coach P is going to be really mad," Boeheim said of the SU football coach, "but, Donovan, I need you for another week."

This team was built, strand by strand, like college teams in the 1950s, while the school licked its wounds and recovered from probation. This is our team, a regional team, with

JOHN WALLACE CELEBRATES AFTER SU'S VICTORY AGAINST KANSAS IN THE NCAA TOURNAMENT.

SYRACUSE BASKETBALL: A CENTURY OF MEMORIES

kids who went to high school within driving distance. Hill is from White Plains, Wallace from Rochester, Janulis for Prattsburg, Cipolla from Queens.

And Sims, the guy who runs it all, came up from Kirk Park.

The eeriest thing about the game came with 13 seconds left, SU up by two and taking the ball out: Sims stepped from the huddle grinning and laughing to himself. Last summer, he nearly left the sport when he lost his dad. Last week, while on the road, his grandfather died, and his mother broke the news to him when he came back home. Now his team was holding on by the skin of its teeth, and he walked onto the court with a smile on his face.

SU held on, and Sims knelt on the court and prayed.

"Praise God," said Sims, explaining that smile. "I knew we were going to win. I just knew."

He knew because this team was knit together, strand by strand.

game summary | march 24, 1996

SYRACUSE (60)

	fg-fga	ft-fta	r	a	pts
Burgan	3-11	2-7	8	1	8
Wallace	5-16	4-6	9	1	15
Hill	5-10	5-7	6	0	15
Sims	0-4	4-4	4	4	4
Cipolla	4-9	1-2	2	2	11
Janulis	0-1	1-2	2	1	1
Patrick	0-0	0-0	0	0	0
Reafsnyder	3-5	0-0	5	0	6
Team			8		
Totals	20-56	17-28	44	9	60

KANSAS (57)

	fg-fga	ft-fta	r	a	pts
Pierce	3-9	4-5	7	0	11
La Frentz	3-8	0-1	9	0	6
Pollard	5-9	0-1	7	0	10
Vaughn	8-12	2-2	3	4	21
Haase	0-9	3-4	3	6	3
Williams	2-4	0-0	5	0	4
Pugh	0-3	0-0	3	0	0
Robertson	1-3	0-0	4	2	2
Pearson	0-2	0-0	0	1	0
Rayford	0-0	0-0	1	0	0
Thomas	0-5	0-0	0	0	0
Team			3		
Totals	22-64	9-13	45	13	57

Halftime score: Syracuse 35, Kansas 26. Officials: Don Rutledge, Larry Rose and Frank Scagliotta. Technical Fouls: 0. Attendance: 17,074.

statistics

It's No Joke:
This SU Team Riding High

MARCH 31, 1996 | BY BUD POLIQUIN, THE POST-STANDARD

It is the team that couldn't . . . wouldn't . . . shouldn't. A team which had been plopped in nobody's Top 25 polls back in late autumn. A team coached by a man who for too long has had to answer for his temperament rather than for his triumphs.

And now it is bound for the very place where basketball dreams can come true, where legends are made and where tears of happiness tend to roll down cheeks.

Hey, it's no early April Fool's Day joke. The Syracuse University Orangemen, a gutty group that knocked off Mississippi State here Saturday evening, 77-69, will play for the national championship before tens of millions of viewers Monday night.

And now, who dares to insist they cannot win the whole thing?

"We've been the underdog since the tournament started," John Wallace observed after his club had played its way into the Final Two. "That has no effect on us. We don't care about that. The other teams pull up their shorts the same as us. We don't care if people don't think we can win. As long as we think we can win, that's all that matters."

Understand that these Orangemen—who are nothing if not a splendid mix of brain, brawn and grit—think they can beat any group that dares to stand before them. And why not? SU has now swept Montana State and Drexel and Georgia and Kansas and Mississippi State out of this NCAA Tournament. Fairly easily, too, with the exception of that overtime tong war with Georgia.

And while all that may be viewed as a most improbable march by so many across the land, there is nobody in the Syracuse party who would agree. Especially now.

Why, to get to the brink, to put itself in this position to win the school's first-ever national championship in basketball, SU merely had to upset the very Mississippi State squad that had beaten Kentucky, Connecticut and Cincinnati this month alone.

No matter, though. Boeheim merely did what Rick Pitino, Jim Calhoun and Bob Huggins—all more celebrated coaches than the Syracuse bossman—could not do. Namely, he orchestrated a perfect game plan that toppled the very Bulldogs squad that had become this tournament's colossus.

First of all, Boeheim threw his now-feared "2-3" zone at Mississippi State, which responded to it like five guys raking leaves in the wind by ham-handedly turning the ball over a stunning 21 times, including nine alone by Bulldog point guard Marcus Bullard.

SU's 1995-1996 NCAA finals team.

Then, at the other end of the court, the coach took a look at MSU's 6-foot-11, 265-pound center, Erick Dampier—biceps and all—and ordered his athletes to take the ball right at him. Wallace . . . Otis Hill . . . Todd Burgan. Didn't matter. Under instructions from Boeheim, each saddled up and rode down the lane at the big man, who proved to be more body than barrier.

The result was one blocked shot (and few altered ones) by Dampier, a kid with arms as long as snow shovels who rarely bothered to raise them. Perhaps, though, all that sinew is hard to lift.

In any event, Syracuse—which made but five turnovers in the entire game—pretty much performed like a club used to the dealings of bright lights and every-shot importance. The Bulldogs, on the other hand, played like a nervous little team from Mayberry, North Carolina, Or Starkville, Mississippi. Same thing.

This, then, can be credited to Boeheim, yes? Well, no. Not according to him, anyway.

"I don't understand the tournament, exactly," he said after nevertheless running his record in it to 20-8 over the past seven seasons. "It's too hard to figure this tournament out, as much as you'd like to think you've got an idea. I don't know if any of us have figured it out yet."

Clearly, it appears that he has. Three of those eight tournament losses, remember, have come in overtime. To Massachusetts in Worcester four years ago. To Missouri in Los Angeles two years ago. To Arkansas in Austin, Texas, one year ago.

Anybody else spot a trend here? Simply,

Boeheim's Orangemen, as tough as cheap steaks in bad restaurants at this point in the calendar, are nobody to draw in the early spring. And the fact of the matter is this: The coach fully expects them to prove that again Monday night.

"The kids play hard," Boeheim said of his Orangemen, now 29-8 and proving they are anything but the fourth-best team in the Big East Conference. "They play together. They look for each other. And they're not afraid to step up."

Neither are they timid in their celebration. Wallace, as is his wont, often woofed on the floor at MSU's Dontae Jones en route to his game-high 21 points. Lazarus Sims, brilliant with nine assists and no turnovers, stomped about with the I-can-lick-any-man-in-the-house glower on his way to and from time-outs and fired the game ball into the stands at the buzzer. Donovan McNabb and Elimu Nelson, the bench jockeys, worked their usual body-language magic throughout the night.

And then there was Jason Cipolla, the hometown kid who scored all nine of his points in the second half, and then down the stretch—with time still on the clock—picked up a courtside telephone and began to chat to whomever may have been on the other end.

"The phone thing?" he asked. "I was just reaching out and telling them we were going to the finals. To the championship game."

Unbelievable, isn't it? Remarkable. The team that wouldn't . . . couldn't . . . shouldn't is 40 minutes removed from a title. Which means Cipolla's was no stupid telephone prank. Which further means SU's funky theme song has got it right.

April is about to dawn, and the 'Cuse is still in the house. Imagine that.

BURGAN GETS WORDS
OF EXPERIENCE

MARCH 31, 1996 | BY DAVID RAMSEY, SYRACUSE HERALD AMERICAN

East Rutherford, N.J.—Derrick Coleman left his home in Philadelphia Thursday evening and took a drive to New York City.

He had a lecture appointment with Todd Burgan. He stopped at the Embassy Suites Hotel where the Orangemen are staying for the Final Four. He sat down with John Wallace, who wears Coleman's No. 44, Lazarus Sims and Burgan, an old friend from Detroit. The foursome talked from 11 p.m. until 2:30 in the morning.

"Y'all have an opportunity to do something amazing," Coleman said, "something I never achieved."

Coleman earns several million to play basketball for the 76ers. But he can't purchase an NCAA title. He came achingly close in 1987 when SU fell to Indiana.

He turned to Burgan.

"You're able to get to the basket on your drives, " Coleman said, "but you're finessing it. You're not driving with confidence. You own the hole on Saturday. You own it!

"If you don't finish strong on those drives, you're seeing me afterward."

Sims and Wallace laughed heartily. Burgan didn't even crack a smile.

"He knew," Coleman said, "I was serious."

On Saturday evening in the Meadowlands, Burgan finally chuckled about his meeting with Coleman.

"Yeah, he threatened me," Burgan said. Coleman and Burgan grew up in the same Detroit neighborhood. Harsh words are common, a fact of the territory.

"He threatened," Burgan said again. "That encouraged me."

Burgan, who struggled in Denver, ripped his way to 19 points, seven rebounds and even sank five-of-six from the free-throw line. He is one of the prime reasons the Orangemen will play Monday in the title game.

It was a joyous week in Syracuse for most. It was a harsh week for Burgan.

First, he had to deal with himself.

"I'm my own toughest critic," he said as he punched himself in the chest with startling force. "I really wanted to get ready for this game. I had to make up for what could have been."

MEMBERS OF THE 1995-96 FINALS TEAM CELEBRATE A WIN OVER MISSISSIPPI STATE IN THE NCAAs.

What could have been.

That was the second problem. He had to deal with those who just had to remind him of his free-throw woes. Burgan missed three free throws in the late moments against Kansas. It only took 17 seconds. The shots could have cost the Orangemen this trip to Jersey.

"People were telling me about those shots all week," Burgan said.

"I got sick of it. The only way to shut them up is to make them."

He began the silencing act immediately.

Erick Dampier, Mississippi State's center, is an extremely large human being, the kind of man who could send a chill through the heart of Goliath.

Three minutes into the game, Burgan roared down the lane and rose into the sky. He was defying Dampier. He was doing exactly what Coleman had commanded.

He slammed.

Boom. One question had been answered. Burgan would have nothing to do with timidity on this evening.

Next came the more subtle answer.

With three minutes left and the game still in doubt, Burgan went to the line to shoot free throws.

He is a difficult player to read. He wears a perpetual look of gloom on the court. He wore it at the line against Kansas. He wore it again Saturday.

He swished both free throws. Mississippi State was deceased.

When the final horn sounded, Burgan pounded his chest with left hand. He looked into the stands, to the ninth row. He pounded his chest, and he kept looking.

He saw his father, Lamont, and his brother, Lamont II. They, too, were pounding their chests. They were rattling the bones that protect the heart.

"He's got heart," said Lamont, beaming with pride. "He's got that toughness."

Years ago, Lamont II took little brother to the playgrounds of Detroit. They usually played behind Cody High School on Cathedral Street.

The rules were simple. Get beat, sit down and wait a long time for the next game. Expect to catch a lot of elbows. Expect to fall to the concrete floor.

"It makes you tough," Lamont II said. "You can't lose. You can't sit down.

"He had to grow up. If he didn't take care of himself. I would have to fight for him. I'm the big brother. I couldn't let anybody push Todd around.

"He learned endurance. He learned perseverance. He learned the game."

Lamont II has nothing to worry about now. His brother, the one who will play for the title Monday, needs no defender. He is the most rugged, most ruthless member of this surprising team.

He listened to big brother. He listened to Big Derrick.

And then he carried his team to the biggest game.

game summary | march 30, 1996

MISSISSIPPI STATE (69)

	m	fg-fga	ft-fta	r	pf	a	pts
Walters	32	5-9	0-0	6	5	0	10
Jones	37	6-16	2-2	6	4	2	16
Dampier	36	4-6	4-4	14	1	6	12
Bullard	39	4-9	0-0	5	2	8	11
Wilson	37	7-16	0-0	2	4	3	20
Hughes	10	0-0	0-0	5	0	1	0
Washington	4	0-0	0-0	1	1	0	0
Hyche	5	0-0	0-0	1	1	1	0
Team				1			
Totals	200	26-56	6-6	41	18	21	69

SYRACUSE (77)

	m	fg-fga	ft-fta	r	pf	a	pts
Burgan	39	6-11	5-6	7	1	2	19
Wallace	40	6-14	8-10	4	2	2	21
Hill	32	7-11	1-2	2	4	1	15
Sims	40	3-5	4-4	5	2	9	11
Cipolla	32	3-9	2-2	1	0	1	9
Reafsnyder	8	1-3	0-0	2	1	0	2
Janulis	9	0-1	0-0	0	1	0	0
Team				0			
Totals	200	26-55	20-24	21	11	10	77

Halftime: Syracuse 36, Mississippi State 36; Technical Fouls: 0; Officials: Frank Scagliotta, Andre Pattillo and Mike Sanzere; Attendance: 19,229

statistics

137

Number One
In Our Hearts

Orangemen Gave 'Everything They Had'

APRIL 2, 1996 | BY DONNA DITOTA, SYRACUSE HERALD-JOURNAL

East Rutherford, N.J.— John Wallace couldn't watch.

The Syracuse University forward had spent the final minute and six seconds of the NCAA championship game on the Orange sideline, a green towel stretched over his head. He had scored a game-high 29 points and hauled in 10 rebounds before a fifth and disqualifying foul sentenced him to the bench. He had almost brought his Orangemen, a team that finished fourth in the Big East this season, a team most considered a mere footnote in Kentucky's self-fulfilling prophecy, to the brink of heaven.

But here, on a late Monday night in New Jersey, Wallace couldn't bear to witness what might have been.

The Kentucky Wildcats won college basketball's national title, beating the Orangemen, 76-67. They cut down the nets, substituted "UK" for "The 'Cuse" in SU's triumphant Denver rap song, and pulled on their commemorative hats and T-shirts.

Wallace never saw it. He climbed over the Orange bench and escaped into the SU locker room, that towel draped across his shoulders.

On the court, Otis Hill stood doubled-over at the free throw line, his hands covering his face. Lazarus Sims sat nearby, his legs splayed in front of him, two teammates' huddled around him offering consolation.

"The worst feeling I ever had," Hill and Sims said later, both excluding the days their fathers died.

In one corner of the Continental Airlines Arena, however, Todd Burgan stood, one hand on his hip, the other wrapped around a water bottle, Burgan watched as Kentucky players gleefully embraced, Kentucky fans celebrated and the arena maintenance crew erected the platform to have the Wildcats receive their championship hardware.

Burgan watched and tried to sort out his thoughts.

"I was just thinking about all the hard work in the preseason, all the weightlifting, all the running to get to this point.

"We didn't get over the hump and win the national championship, but I was proud." Burgan said. "You have a lot of mixed emotions, but you have to be very, very proud because there were a lot of teams that were home just wishing they could be in this position.

138

"Probably, it'll hit me later on and I'll really be disappointed, but right now, I'm proud. I'm not satisfied, but I'm proud."

The Orangemen had reason to be.

SU shot 50 percent against the nation's best team and held those same Wildcats to 38 percent from the floor.

The Orangemen rallied from a 59-46 deficit when it looked as if the Wildcats might crack the game wide open. They cut the Kentucky lead to two and gave themselves a chance at a title.

Hill soared for an offensive rebound and slammed. Sims penetrated and found Wallace, who dunked. Burgan drilled an open three-pointer.

And Wallace, the All-American, did what he's done best all season. He took over the game.

He started at the free-throw line and waltzed through the lane, dunking and drawing a foul. He shimmied beneath the basket and chest-bumped his teammates. The score was 62-58; two minutes later, Wallace struck again.

This time, he spun with balletic grace on the baseline and deposited a layup. Rick Pitino later rated Wallace's championship performance "terrific" and predicted Wallace would win the NBA's rookie of the year award next season.

But for now, Wallace was merely keeping his team alive. SU trailed, 64-62, with 4:46 left in the game. The Orangemen were in it. The Orangemen would not die.

"We put ourselves in position to win the basketball game," SU coach Jim Boeheim said. "And Kentucky made great plays."

The Wildcats' next two plays epitomized the way they beat SU Monday. Walter McCarty tipped in a missed Kentucky three-pointer, one of 18 offensive rebounds the Wildcats corralled. On Kentucky's next possession, the Wildcats got penetration against SU's stalwart zone and kicked the ball out to Derek Anderson, who drained a three-pointer, one of 12 Kentucky made.

SU's John Wallace covers his face after he fouled out in the NCAA basketball title game at the Meadowlands.

The 24 Orange turnovers, too, contributed to SU's demise.

The end finally came on one of those miscues when Sims penetrated, searching for Wallace, and Mark Pope swiped at the pass. Boeheim later called the steal "the game play."

Wallace fouled, his fifth, and even though he gathered his teammates and delivered another of his pep talks about believing in themselves, it looked unlikely when Pope drained both those free throws.

"Every time we got within two or four points," Sims said, "they hit a three or got an offensive rebound. And that set us back, for the simple fact we were playing so hard to get in that position."

With 43.2 seconds left, Boeheim stood with his toes touching the stripe of the coach-

139

SYRACUSE (67)   KENTUCKY (76)

	m	fg	ft-fta	o-reb	pf	a	pts		m	fg	ft-fta	o-reb	pf	a	pts
Burgan	38	7-10	2-5	2-8	5	1	19	Anderson	16	4-8	1-1	3-4	2	1	11
Wallace	38	11-19	5-5	3-10	5	1	29	Walker	32	4-12	3-8	4-9	2	4	11
Hill	28	3-9	1-1	2-10	2	1	7	McCarty	19	2-6	0-0	5-7	3	3	4
Sims	39	2-5	1-2	1-2	2	7	6	Delk	37	8-20	1-2	1-7	2	2	24
Cipolla	35	3-8	0-0	0-1	1	2	6	Epps	35	0-6	0-0	1-4	1	7	0
Reafsnyder	13	0-1	0-0	0-4	0	0	1 0	Pope	27	1-6	2-2	1-3	3	2	4
Janulis	8	0-0	0-0	0-2	2	0	0	Mercer	24	8-12	1-1	1-2	3	2	20
Nelson	1	0-0	0-0	0-0	0	0	0	Sheppard	7	1-2	0-1	1-2	3	0	2
								Edwards	3	0-1	0-0	0-0	0	1	0
Totals	200	26-52	9-13	8-38	17	12	67	Totals	200	28-73	8-13	18-40	19	22	76

Halftime: Kentucky 42-33; Technical fouls: 0; Fouled Out: Wallace, Burgan, Syracuse; Officials: John Clougherty, Scott Thornley, David Libbey

ing box, his arms folded in front of him. He stood, frozen, for about 20 seconds.

His team trailed by seven, its championship hopes receding. The SU cheering section, only minutes earlier bursting with Orange pompons and hopeful chants of "Let's Go Orange," stood mostly silent and spent.

Later, when the nets had come down, Wallace and Sims visited the Kentucky locker room to offer congratulations. Boeheim spoke by telephone to President Clinton and told him these Orangemen were the "best group I've ever had."

There had been hope, there had been talk of a national championship and of gathering at City Hall today to celebrate the triumph.

In the end came defeat. But for SU players and coaches, too, it was topped with a dollop of vindication.

They finished the year 29-9 and competed on the season's last day. And as much as they had dreamed of hoisting high that championship trophy, No. 2 couldn't be all bad.

"They should be as proud as Kentucky is," Boeheim said. "They gave everything they had, and that, as a coach, is all you can ask for."

THE TEAM'S CREED WAS NEVER 'CLOSE ENOUGH'

APRIL 2, 1996 | BY SEAN KIRST, THE POST-STANDARD

East Rutherford, N.J.—Be careful with this team. Be careful what you say. They are kids, young men. They do not, and cannot, understand—at least not yet.

Be careful with this team. If you see the players in a mall or on a street, be careful in the way you phrase your good intentions. They will not want congratulations, because they lost the game. At this minute, in their bellies, they feel they should have won.

They are kids, young men. It will take them a while to see what they did in the Meadowlands.

You and I know what we saw, along with millions of others. Kentucky defeated Syracuse University on Monday, 76-67. We saw an undersized team that went only seven deep going up against a fast and strong basketball machine. We saw young men who were bent over, cramping with fatigue, who had chance after chance to simply cave in. We saw a kid from our town who will now pass into legend, Lazarus Sims, fall hard on his wrist, tape it tight and then keep playing.

But the Orangemen themselves will not hold up those things. "I think we played very good," said John Wallace, who scored 29 points before fouling out. "We should have won this game."

That was not bitterness, or a losing team's bravado. That belief is why he got here, playing in this game. This Syracuse team had its own private joke, the reason Wallace was smiling at the opening tip, the reason Sims throughout the game would crack unexpected grins. They were not playing for the city of Syracuse. They were not playing to avenge Keith Smart's shot.

They were playing, as Sims said on the eve of the game, for themselves. They had bonded, grown together, to prove all of us wrong. No one had believed in them from the first game on. They were a nice bunch of gamers built around one superstar. But they knew they could play. They believed they could play. In the end, they went on this NCAA run to remember. In their minds, at this point, they did not complete that run.

That is why Otis Hill doubled over in grief, why Wallace turned his back on a crowd of reporters, why Sims walked into the locker room head down. "I've been fortunate to have guys on this team that I love like family," Hill said. This was not the way, inside the team, they saw the family breaking up.

So be careful in what you say to them. They will remember exactly all the things we remember, the four or five plays their coach said decided the whole game.

They will remember, late in the second half, how they closed within two points. They will remember how they closed within 72-67 with less than two minutes to go, and then got back the ball and lost it beneath the hoop. They will remember every free throw they missed, every chance they had to pad an early lead. They will remember every call they felt went the wrong way.

In a year, or maybe five years, they will come to understand. They are kids who came so close in a game that meant it all, so for now it is impossible to take in the whole picture. How they changed the whole perception of a school so many fans found arrogant. The way they took hold of so many people's hopes,

with their team hugs and their rap song and they way they shared the ball.

And beyond it all they lifted the image of their coach, took Jim Boeheim from a caricature out beyond his own city, and taught people how this guy could make great things from five great hearts.

They can't. They can't understand. It is too early. There is a story you should know about John Wallace, which happened right after the loss by a fingernail to Arkansas a year ago. He was eating dinner in a Syracuse restaurant, and people kept stopping by to congratulate him on his great game. Wallace abruptly looked at his companion, puzzled and upset, and said, "But we lost!"

He is a kid, full of fire, and he can't comprehend. That will come. It will come as he moves on and becomes an adult, as he realizes some words have more than one definition. Like courage, and winning, and what it means to be a champ. The Orangemen have earned that right, but don't tell that to them now.

MARIUS THE MAN FOR SU

MARCH 14, 1998 | BY MIKE WATERS, POST-STANDARD

Lexington, Ky.—Todd Burgan said he would trust Marius Janulis with one shot to win or lose a game even if his fellow senior was 0-for-10 leading up to the big shot.

That trust was tested Friday as Syracuse fought off upset-minded Iona 63-61 in the first round of the NCAA Tournament at Rupp Arena.

Janulis had missed all but one of the seven shots he had attempted in the second half of the game. But with time running out and Syracuse trailing 61-60, Burgan recaptured his own blocked shot and spotted Janulis at the top of the key.

"At first, I was going to get back to the basket," Burgan said. "Then I saw Marius wide open. That was the best decision right there."

Janulis' three-point shot fell through with 1.2 seconds remaining. As the ball arched toward the basket, Janulis backpedaled downcourt with his right hand still in the follow-through position. He brought his hand back up and shot his index finger into the air.

After a timeout, Syracuse's Etan Thomas batted away a last-gasp length-of-the-court pass by Iona's Tariq Kirksay to hold on to the exhilarating win.

"It came down to one shot," coach Jim Boeheim said. "We had the ball last and knocked it in. That was the ball game."

Janulis finished with 14 points that was highlighted by 4-for-7 shooting from three-point range. Burgan led Syracuse with 16 points, while Jason Hart added 15 points, five assists and six steals. Thomas had six blocked shots to break SU's single-season record, held by Derrick Coleman. Thomas now has 131 rejections to Coleman's 127.

Iona, which was led by Kashif Hameed's 17 points, finished its season with a 27-6 record. Syracuse (25-8) advances to the tournament's second round where it will face New Mexico, a 79-62 winner over Butler Friday, at approximately 2:30 p.m. Sunday.

The final minutes were a series of momentum shifts. Hameed dropped a tricky reverse layup with 1:26 remaining as the Gaels took a 58-57 lead. Janulis then dropped in a three-pointer with time running out on the 35-second shot clock. It was his first basket in 30 minutes of play.

"The one in the corner, that's about as tough a shot as you can have," Boeheim said of the three-pointer. "He hadn't made anything, I think, in the second half. To step up and

143

make that shot, there aren't many people who can do that. But he had to take it. The shot clock was running down."

SU's 60-58 lead held up for less than 30 seconds. John McDonald, Iona's spunky point guard, nailed an answering three-pointer for a 61-60 lead with 24 seconds left.

That set the stage for the wild sequence at the end of the game.

Jason Hart tried to drive into the lane but was walled off. He passed to Ryan Blackwell, who handed off to Burgan with 10 seconds to go. Burgan tried to get to the basket. He was closely guarded by Iona's Donell Mitchell. Hameed came over to help and blocked Burgan's shot.

Burgan retrieved the ball and fired it outside.

"I've been with Marius for four years," Burgan said. "He's the best shooter I've ever been around. If Marius goes 0-for 10, when he gets the ball the next time I believe it's going to go in. I have supreme confidence in him. We'll take that shot every time."

Janulis was not where he would normally be, which is on the wing or in the corner. He had drifted to the top of the key as Burgan drove down the right side of the lane.

"I was supposed to be on the weak side," Janulis said, "looking for somebody to drive, and if they got double-teamed then I would get the ball. Todd made a great play, and I just happened to be wide open."

Iona coach Tim Welsh said he knew Janulis was the last player to leave unguarded. Welsh, a former SU assistant, had seen the Orangemen play in the Big East Tournament where Janulis made 7-of-11 three-pointers.

"There's no way we'd ever leave Janulis that wide open in a regular set." Welsh said. "We made the last shot, but we didn't get the loose ball. Sometimes the worst thing that can happen is a blocked shot because it takes your defense out of position."

That's exactly what happened, according to Kirksay, who had been guarding Janulis.

"I felt we did a great job of helping on Burgan," Kirksay said. "We got the block and I lost sight of my man. When Burgan got the ball back, I couldn't get back."

The Orangemen were the ones trying to get back after blowing a 10-point lead in the first half. Syracuse committed 14 turnovers in the first half, but gave the ball away just six times in the second half. Iona fell behind early as it missed 13 of its first 15 shots. The Gaels eventually pulled to within 30-29 at halftime.

The Gaels jumped on the Orangemen to start the second half. Hart had two steals to help Syracuse rally. He turned both into easy layups. One came with SU trailing 45-39 midway through the second half, and the other came after a controversial double-foul gave Iona the ball with a 56-55 lead and 2:20 remaining.

"It was one of those games where we were able to stay close," Hart said. "We expect Todd and Marius to make plays like that. They're our seniors."

In the end, the game and Syracuse's season came down to the two senior co-captains, Burgan and Janulis.

"When Todd threw the ball out to him, I was just worried about what was going to be left on the clock," Boeheim said. "I felt he'd make that shot. He hit the rim, which he doesn't usually do, but we'll take it."

144

HUSKIES SKUNKED

SU HUMBLES UNDERMANNED CONNECTICUT

FEBRUARY 2, 1999 | BY MIKE WATERS, THE POST-STANDARD

Hartford, Conn.—The Syracuse Orangemen beat the nation's top-ranked team. Three-fifths of the nation's top-ranked team, anyway.

Syracuse defeated No. 1 ranked and previously unbeaten Connecticut 59-42 at the Hartford Civic Center Monday night. However, two of Connecticut's starters missed the game due to injuries.

Connecticut played without All-America candidate Richard Hamilton and starting center Jake Voskuhl. Both players suffered injuries in UConn's 78-74 win over St. John's on Saturday. Hamilton, the Big East's leading scorer at 22.1 points per game, is listed as day-to-day with a deep thigh bruise. Voskuhl, a 6-foot-11 junior and UConn's leading rebounder, is out indefinitely with a stress fracture in his left foot.

Given the opportunity, the Orangemen avoided a letdown against an undermanned opponent and held the Huskies to their lowest total ever in a Big East Conference game. The 42 points were the fewest scored by a Syracuse opponent since the Big East began in 1979.

"I told the players before the game, 'This is a hard adjustment for us,' " SU coach Jim Boeheim said. "We have to go out there and play. We can't be concerned with who's there and who's not there. We need to get wins. This was a huge win for us."

UConn coach Jim Calhoun made no excuses. Even though the Huskies lost 28 points and 12 rebounds with Hamilton and Voskuhl sidelined, his team's lack of effort disappointed Calhoun. Syracuse outrebounded Connecticut 37-26 and forced the Huskies into 18 turnovers.

"We had five people dressed who could play," Calhoun said. "I thought it would have been more competitive. They played with more vigor, they got us on the backboards, they got to loose balls, which really, really drives me crazy."

The Orangemen (16-6, 7-5) beat a Top 10 team for the first time since knocking off No. 4 Kansas in the 1996 NCAA Tournament's West Region finals. Connecticut (19-1 overall, 11-1 in the Big East) became the last Division 1 team to lose a game this season.

No Hamilton. No Voskuhl. No matter. To Syracuse, the win tasted just as sweet. The Huskies had won 31 straight home games and still had two three-year starters—Kevin Freeman and Ricky Moore—and one two-year starter in 1998 Big East Rookie of the Year Khalid El-Amin.

"We just had to come in here and win whether it was Rutgers, Pitt or Providence," SU junior Jason Hart said. "Granted, Richard Hamilton didn't play, but we still had to come out and get a good victory. I thought we did a great job of not taking them lightly."

SYRACUSE (59)

	fg-fga	ft-fta	r	a	pts
Brown	6-8	0-2	4	0	14
Blackwell	4-10	5-6	6	1	13
Thomas	5-8	2-4	9	1	12
Hart	3-14	0-0	5	3	6
Griffin	4-10	1-1	3	1	12
Shumpert	0-0	0-0	0	0	0
Bland	0-0	0-0	0	0	0
Ovcina	1-4	0-1	2	1	2
Team			5		
Totals	23-54	8-14	37	7	59

KANSAS (42)

	fg-fga	ft-fta	r	a	pts
Jones	1-4	0-0	0	1	2
Freeman	3-9	3-7	8	1	9
Wane	2-2	0-0	2	1	4
Moore	0-1	0-0	1	3	0
El-Amin	2-12	0-0	2	4	6
Klaiber	0-0	0-0	0	0	0
Mourning	2-7	3-4	4	2	7
Harrison	0-1	0-0	2	1	0
Saunders	6-9	1-1	3	1	14
Team			4		
Totals	16-45	7-12	26	14	42

Halftime score: 25-25. Technicals: 0. Fouled out: 0. Officials: Jim Burr, Bob Donato, and John Clougherty. Attendance: 16,294.

statistics

146

UConn Win Helps Teams in Big East on Bubble

FEBRUARY 7, 1999 | BY BOB SNYDER, SYRACUSE HERALD AMERICAN

Was SU's upset of UConn really the first time the Orangemen ever toppled No. 1? Technically, yes. The AP poll didn't start until 1949.

In the '29-30 season, Doc Carlson's unbeaten Pittsburgh team, acknowledged to be No. 1 in the land and featuring All-American Charley Hyatt, came here to face Lew Andreas' SU squad. More than 3,200 squeezed into Archbold Gym, another 1,000 being turned away. Hyatt was shut down; SU won.

SYRACUSE STARTERS, FROM LEFT, RYAN BLACKWELL (32), JASON HART (5), AND ETAN THOMAS, ALONG WITH COACH JIM BOEHEIM, WATCH AS THEIR RESERVE PLAYERS FINISH UP A GAME IN 1999.

AP/WIDE WORLD PHOTOS

147

SYRACUSE ALL-TIME LETTERMEN

1900-1999

A

Ableman, Richard M.	1964-65-66
Ackerson, James	1943
Ackley, Albert	1925
Ackley, Earl E., Jr.	1948-49-50
Acocella, Angelo	1945
Addison, Rafael	1983-84-85-86
Albsmese, Vincent J.	1956-57
Aldrich, David G.	1967-68-69
Alexis, Wendell	1983-84-85-86
Alkoff, Louis	1933-34-35
Amster, Glenn, Jr. (mgr.)	1968-69
Andrew, David (mgr.)	1989
Ansley, Emest C.	1910
Ardison, Robert (mgr.)	1932
Armstrong, George	1930-31-32
Arrington, Larry	1975-76
Austin, Ernest	1968-69-70
A.utry, Adrian	1991-92-93-94
Axelrod, Leonard (mgr.)	1942
Axlmann, O.J. (mgr.)	1914

B

Balinsky, John	1935-36-37
Balukas, Raymond R.	1967-68
Banks, M.B.	1909
Barlok, Todd	1992
Barlow, Michael R.	1968 69
Barnes, Renard	1986
Biarshu John	1918-19-20
Bartholomew, Bruce	1972-73
Baylock, Victor	1936-37-38
Beale, Kenneth	1929-30-31
Beck, lohn F.	1948-49-50
Bednark, Thomas R.	1966-67
Beech, George	1932 33
Begovich, Mike	1994
Beisswanger, Russell W.	1962

Bennett, Milton	1921
Berkenfeld, Stephen M.	1959-60-61
Berger, Eugene	1940-41-42
Besdin, Melvin	1952-53-54
Beverly, Lewis M.	1954
Bibbens, Ross	1921
Biener, Jerald H. (mgr.)	1953-54
Bing, David	1964-65-66
Blackwell, Ryan M.	1998-99
Bland, Tony	1999
Blazey, Scott (mgr.)	1971-72
Bloom, Myer	1911-12-13-14
Blumen, Kyle (mgr.)	1993
Blumen, Todd (mgr.)	1990
Boax, James	1927
Bock, Milton	1931-32-33
Boeheim, James A.	1964-65-66
Boetcher, Maynard	1930
Bohr, F.M.	1903
Bolton, William	1940
Bouie, Roosevelt	1977-78-79-80
Boyce, Richard L. (mgr.)	1960-61
Brady, E.J.	1903
Breland, Emanuel F.	1954-55-57
Brenneman, George	1929
Brickman, H.	1918
Brodsky, Jon D. (mgr.)	1958
Brodsky, William J. (mgr.)	1964-65
Bromberg, Fred	1931
Brower, Derek A.	1985-86-87-88
Brown, Damone L.	1998-99
Brown, James N.	1955-56
Brown. Melvin	1985-86
Brown, Michael	1985
Brown, Willis (mgr.)	1932
Brucker, Joseph	1922
Bruett, William	1941
Bruin, Tony	1980-81-82-83
Burgan, Todd	1995-96-97-98

149

Dwayne "Pearl" Washington, letterwinner, 1984-85-86

Byrnes, Martin W.   1975-76-77-78

C

Campbell, Malik	1998-99
Carello, Sam (mgr.)	1987
Carr, Harlan	1925
Case, William R	1968-69-70
Casey, James	1916-17
Castellini, August	1954-55
Castle, Lewis S.	1911-12-13-14
Catchpole, Park (mgr.)	1940
Cegala, Louis	1954-55-56
Celluk, Billy	1999
Cheney, Guy W.	1908
Chudy, Peter K.	1959-60-61
Chureh, Lewis W. (mgr.)	1924
Cincebox, W. Jon	1957-58-59
Clark, David L.	1973
Clark, Gary L.	1955-56-57
Clark, Robert (mgr.)	1927
Clary, Robert	1968-69-70
Coffee, Jack (mgr.)	1933
Coffman, David (mgr.)	1938
Cohen, Ronald P. (mgr.)	1965
Cohen, Hal	1977-78-79-80
Cohen, Vincent	1955-56-57
Cohen, Jr., Vincent	1992
Coleman, Derrick D	1987-88-84-90
Coman, A.P. (mgr.)	1916
Conderman, Joseph (mgr.)	1920
Conlin, Frank	1919-20-21
Connors, William J.	1961
Conover, Richard	1958-59-60
Cornwall, Richard T.	1966-67-68
Cosentino, Rudolph	1945
Cotton, Lewis D.	1973
Cracker, William (mgr.)	1926
Crandall, Lawrence	1946-47-48
Crisp, Wilbur	1914-15-16-17
Crofoot, George	1958
Cronauer, Ed	1918
Cronauer, John	1918
Cubit, Mark	1978-79
Cummings, Charles F. (mgr.)	1911
Curran, Jack	1936

D

Danforth, Michael R.	1976
Darby, Walter A.	1909
Davey, Walter V.	1411-12

Davis, Ernest R.	1961
Davis, Ken	1979-80-81
Dean, Herbcrt	1939
Dean, Richard I.	1965-66-67
Deer, A. Carmine	1948-49-50
DeFillippo, Tony	1929
Degner, Donald L.	1973-74-75
Delp, M.Z. (mgr.)	1909
DeMarle, William	1974-75
DeYoung, John	1933-34-35
Dickie, William	1945
DiPace, Daniel	1941-42-43
Dodge, Stephen B.	1962
Dollard, E.A.	1905-06-07-08
Dollard, Edmund (mgr.)	1939
Dolley, Charles	1917-18-19
Dooms, Robert A.	1972-73-74
Douglas, Sherman	1986-87-88-89
Drake, Nancy (mgr.)	1998
Dressler, Frederic (mgr.)	1962-63
Elrew, William	1977-78
Duffy, Richard M.	1963-64-65
Duncan, James Earl	1958
Duncan, G.O.L	1909
DuVal, Dennis	1972-73-74

E

Edwards, Michael E.	1990-91-92-93
Egan, Patrick	1932
Eisemann, William	1926-27
Elliott, Alton	1930-31-32
Ellis, LeRon P.	1990-91
Evans, Gary	1957

F

Face, Charles F.	1923
Farnsworth, Alton	1935
Farrell, S.A.	1907
Fash, William, O.	1948-49-50
Feldman, Dan	1931
Ferris, Paul	1943
Ferris, William	1934
Fine, Bernard A. (mgr.)	1966-67
Finley, Robert C.	1962-63
Finney, William	1969-70-72
Fisher, George	1921-22-23
Fisher, W. Claude	1909
Fitzpatrick, Richard	1933
Flynn, Raymond	1946
Fogarty, Daniel	1929-30-31

151

WENDELL ALEXIS, LETTERWINNER, 1983-84-85-86

Foster, Herbert	1962-63	Healy, Willard (mgr.)	1941
Frank, Mike (mgr.)	1995	Henderson, Jack (mgr.)	1936
Frazier, Erik	1996-97	Hennemuth, William	1945
Fredericks, Paul	1907	Hicker, George P.	1967-68
		Hill, Otis	1994-95-96-97
		Hladik, Anthony, Jr.	1949-50-51
		Holbrook, Bernard	1930

G

Gabor, William	1945-46-47-48	Hollenbeck, David A.	1958
Gallivan, John F.	1923	Hopkins, Michael C.	1990-91-92-93
Gelatt, Charles	1994	Hom, Harry	1938-89
Getzfeld, Robert (mgr.)	1946-47	Horowitz, Paul	1928
Giles, Clarence W.	1911	Houseknecht, C.J.	1903
Gillespie, Ronald C.	1954-55-56	Howard, LaSean	1997-98
Gipson, Bernard F.	1968-69	Hudson, Joseph (mgr.)	1935
Glacken, Edward	1947	Huggins, Eric H.	1950-51-52
Glacken, Joseph	1942-43-47	Hughes, Keith	1987
Gluck, Jason	1994	Hutt, Less (mgr.)	1928
Gluckman, Harold (mgr.)	1939-40		
Gobobe, Zangwill	1930		
Goercki, John	1936-37-38		

J

Goldberg, Edward D.	1958-59-60	Jackson III, Lucious B.	1992-93-94-95
Goldman, Scott (mgr.)	1990	Jaffe, Myron T.	1950
Goldsmith, Norman B.	1964-65-66	James, Kevin O.	1976-77-78
Gordon, Sidney (mgr.)	1931	James, Loren O.	1961
Green, John (mgr.)	1979	Janulis, Marius	1995-96-97-98
Green, Martin A. (mgr.)	1975	Jarvis, George	1947-48-49
Green, Thomas M.	1969-70-71	Jaskot, Richard C.	1954
Greenman, Lloyd	1919	Jensen, Richard	1939-40
Greve, Henry	1923-24-25	Jerebko, Christopher	1978-79-80-81
Griffin, Allen L.	1998-99	Jockle, Thomas	1950-51
Guerrero, Gilbert	1970	Johnson, Dave M.	1939-90-91-92
Guley, Marcel	1935-36	Johnson, Derrick	1995
		Jones, Stuart (mgr.)	1959
		Jordan, John	1972

H

K

Hackett, Rudolph	1973-74-75		
Haley, Robert (mgr.)	1933		
Haller, Mark	1938-39	Karpis, John	1983-84
Hamblen, Frank A. II	1967 63-69	Kartluke, Paul	1939-40-41
Hanson, Victor A.	1925-26-27	Kasbar, Brenda (rngr.)	1990
Harmon, David	1969-70	Kates, Bernard	1923
Harper, Vaughn	1966-67-68	Katz, Everett	1931
Harned, Herman	1986-87-88-89	Katz, Joel	1985-86-87
Harris, Anthony E.	1992	Katz, Lawrence D.	1967
Harris, Kenneth	1916	Katz, Milton	1931
Hart, Jason K.	1997-98-99	Keating, D.J.	1910
Harwood, John	1928-29-30	Keating, Steven	1992
Hauck, Walter (mgr.)	1976	Keefer, Ralph	1917
Hawkins, Andre	1932-33-34-35	Keib, J.E.	1915
Hayman, Louis	1929-30-31	Kelley, Lawrance	1975-76-77
Hayes, Jim	1994-95-96	Kellogg, William	1922
Headd, Martin	1978-79-80-81	Kerins, Sean	1981-82-83-84

BILLY OWENS, LETTERWINNER, 1989-90-91

Kernan, James	1919		
Keys, William	1976-77		
Kiley, John F.	1949-50-51	Machemer, Fred E.	1960-61-62
Kilpatrick, John	1909-10	Mackey, John	1961
Kilpatrick, Ronald N.	1953	MacNaughton, Donald	1937-38-39
Kindel, Ross	1975-76-77-78	MacRae, Evander G.	1922-23-24
King, Donald A.	1961	Maister, Elmer	1932-33-34
King, Kevin	1974-75-76	Mallin, Jason	1998
Kingsley, J.E.	1912	Manikas, William	1951-52-53
Kinne, Charles C. (mgr.)	1905-06	Manning, Richard A.	1989-90
Kirchgasser, George	1904-05-06	Mantho, Timothy A.	1967
Kline, David	1953-54	Marcus, Abraham	1939
Klutchkowski, Manfred	1962-63	Marcus, Leon	1918-19
Kohls, Gregory	1970-71-72	Marczak, John (mgr.)	1998
Kohm, Joseph	1986-87	Markowitz, Harry (mgr.)	1926
Kollath, D. Bruce	1959-60	Martin, Daniel	1919
Konstanty, Casimer J.	1939	Maxon, H.F. (mgr.)	1913
Kouray, Christian	1940-41	May, James	1994-95-96
Kouwe, Robert L.	1967-69	Mayley, Gordon	1926
Kruse, Stanley	1940-41	McCarthy, C.H	1922
		McCarthy, Charles	1924
		McCorkle, Scott	1991-92-93-94
L		McDaniel, Robert	1970
		McFadden, Gerald	1969-70
Label William (mgr.)	1950	McGough, Michael (mgr.)	1985
Lambert, David (mgr.)	1988	McMillian, J. Paul	1939-40
Lambert, Robert	1928	McNabb, Donovan	1996-97
Lamed, John E	1953-54-55	McRae, Conrad B.	1990-91-92-93
Lavin, Kenneth	1922	McTiernan, Thomas	1943
Lazor, Bobby	1995-96	Meadors, Mark	1974-75
Leavitt, Norman	1936-37-38	Mendell, Irving	1925
Lee, Charles	1925-26-27	Mendelson, Sidney	1924-25
Lee, David F. (mgr.)	1907	Miller, Edwin B.	1950-51-52
Lee, James P.	1973-74-75	Miller, Francis J.	1945-48-49-50
Lee, Matthew T.	1908-09-10	Mogish, Andrew	1943-46-47
Lee, Michael	1971-72-73	Monroe, Greg	1984-85-86-87
Leonard, John	1919	Moss, Eddie	1978-79-80-81
Lewis, Chris	1982-83	Mossey, Thomas E.	1958-59-60
Lighton, Lewis (mgr.)	1925	Moten III, Lawrence E.	1992-93-94-95
Linderman, Peter (mgr.)	1999	Munro, James (mgr.)	1935
Lloyd, Michael	1995	Murray, Robert S.	1962-63-64
Lloyd, Ramel	1997	Mustion, John M.	1960
Lockwood Charles	1994		
Loll, Scott B.	1965		
Lotano, Emest	1961		
Loudis, Laurence G.	1956-57-58	**N**	
Lowe, H.B. (mgr.)	1919		
Lowe W.R.	1922	Nelson, Elimu	1994-95-96
Ludd, Steven O.	1966-67	Nelson, William	1954
Ludka, John	1945-46-47	Newell, Royce	1946-47-48-49
Lynch, Paul	1908	Newton, Lewis	1932
Lyon, F. Murray	1984	Nicoletti, Frank G.	1964-65-66

M

154

STEPHEN D. CANNERELLI, THE SYRACUSE NEWSPAPERS

SHERMAN DOUGLAS, LETTERWINNER, 1986-87-88-89

Niles, Earl B.	1904	Renzi, Oliver	1945-46-47-48
Notman, W.J.	1912-13-14	Rice, E.G.	1903
Noyes, Harold A.	1958-59	Richards, Charles S.	1964-65
		Richtmeyer, Stanley	1926-27-78
		Riehl, A.H.	1912-13

O

		Riehl, Frank H.	1905-06-07-08
O'Byrne, John C. (mgr.)	1914	Riggins, JeCarl	1996-97
O'Connor, Donald (mgr.)	1982-83	Ringelmann, Thomas C.	1966-67
O'Neill, Larry	1981-83	Roche, Robert P.	1951-52
Orr, Louis	1977-78-79-80	Rochester, Stephen S. (mgr.)	1966-67
Osman, A.J.	1915	Roe, Matthew R.	1987-88-89
Osborne, Josh (mgr.)	1922	Rogers, Erik C.	1987-38-39-40
Ovcina, Elvir	1996-97-98-99	Rose, Stanley H. (mgr.)	1952
Owens, William C.	1989-90-91	Rosen, Edward L.	1949-50
		Rosen, Emanuel	1927-28
		Rosser, M.	1927
		Ruby, David (mgr.)	1970

P

		Ruffin, H F.	1917
Parker, Robert M.	1975-76-77	Rugg, W.D.	1911-12
Parker, Wallace	1920-21	Ryan, L.C.	1911-12
Patrick, David	1996		
Patton, Howard (mgr.)	1936		
Payton, Ron	1979-80-81-82		

S

Penceai, Sam	1964-65-66	Santifer, Erich	1980-81-82-83
Perry, Calvin	1980-81-82-83	Saperstein, Gerald	1929
Peters, Roy	1946-47	Sarvay, Merton (mgr.)	1951
Peters, W.L.	1918	Savage, Robert P.	1948-49-50
Phillips, Ronald	1932-33-34	Scherban, Dave (mgr.)	1999
Pickard, Donald	1933-35	Scherban, Mike (mgr.)	1996
Piotrowski, Paul	1970-71-72	Schroeder, John	1937-38-39
Post, Richard (mgr.)	1951	Schubert, William	1946
Potter, A.D.	1915	Schulz, Henry	1947-48-49
Powell, Arthur L	1904-05-06-07	Schwarzer, Joseph	1916-17-18
Powell, Reginald	1976-77	Scott, Oliver	1935-36
Price, Delbert (mgr.)	1942	Scott, Anthony A.	1989-90
Propst, Rudolph W.	1911	Scott, Walter H.	1954
		Scully, John R.	1910
		Seaman, James H.	1962-63

Q

		Sease, Christopher	1974-75-76
Quigley, Terrence J.	1961	Seibert, Ernest R.	1975-76
		Seikaly, Rony F.	1985-86-87-88
		Sekumda, Glenn E.	1992-93
		Semple, Robert (mgr.)	1924-25
		Seymour, R.U.	1913-14-15

R

		Shackleford, Dale P.	1976 77-78-79
Raff, E. (mgr.)	1917	Shaddock, Robert	1942-43
Rafter, William J.	1915-16-17	Shapiro, David (mgr.)	1997
Rakov, Phillip	1925-26	Shaw, Bart	1928-29
Rautins, Leo	1981-82-83	Shaw, Steven	1973-74-75
Reafsnyder, J.B.	1993-94-95-96	Sheehey, Michael	1980-81
Reddout, Franklin P.	1951-52-53	Sherk, Douglas (mgr.)	1977-78
Redlein, George L.	1905-06	Shumpelt, Preston	1999
Reid, Valentine	1965-66		

DERRICK COLEMAN, LETTERWINNER, 1987-88-89-90

Sidat-Singh, Wilmeth	1937-38-39	Thompson, William	1937-38-39
Silverstein, Carl (mgr.)	1950	Thorne, Dudley	1940
Simonaitis, John	1935-36-37	Tichnor, B.C.	1910-11
Sims, Lazarus	1993-94-95-96	Ticktin, Richard (mgr.)	1948-49
Siock, David A.	1989-91-92-93	Timberlake, Chris	1982
Siroty, David (mgr.)	1985	Triche, Howard	1984-85-86-87
Smith, Johrl T. (mgr.)	1923	Trobridge, Rex C	1964-65-66
Smith, William A.	1469-70-71	Trout, Charles	1924
Snyder, James J.	1955-56-57	Twiford, Robert	1939
Solomon, Ira R. (mgr.)	1937	Twombley, E.D.	1903
Sonderman, Edgar	1935-37	Tydeman, William E	1962
Spann, Sam	1998		
Spector, Joseph (mgr.)	1938		
Spencer, Robert S. (mgr.)	1910		

V

Spera, Sonny	1982-83-84-55	Vernick, Carl	1962-63-64
Spicer, Lewis	1945-46	Vogel, Evan	1997
Stanton, Charles	1941-42-43		
Stapleton, S. Scott	1972-73-74		
Stark, J.J.	1905		

W

Stark, Lewis G.	1956	Wadach, Mark	1971-72-73
Stark, Michael	1948-49-50	Waldron, Eugene T.	1981-82-83-84
Stark, Peter G.	1952-53	Walker, Rodney	1986
Stearns, Chester	1931	Walkov, William	1928-29-30
Steams, Robert (mgr.)	1934	Wallace, John	1993-94-95-96
Steere, Robert (mgr.)	1943	Wallach, Robert C.	1948-49-50
Stevesky, Charles	1950-51	Walters, Herbert H. (mgr.)	1915
Stewart, Robert	1937-38-39	Ward, Wayne H.	1968
Stickel, Edward	1946-47-48-49	Warwell, Cliff	1977
Stickney, Russell	1942	Washington, Dwayne	1984-85-86
Stundis, Thomas J.	1972-73-74	Watson, Greg	1982
Suder, John M.	1968-69-70	Watson, Josh	1999
Sugarman, Louis	1908	Weltman, Abraham	1921-22
Suprunowicz, Richard	1949-50-51	Werner, Donald	1940
Suprunowicz, William R.	1973-74	Wichman, Charles	1971-72-73
Swanson, Stanley R.	1951-52	Wiles, Benjamin J. (mgr.)	1937
Sylvester, Joseph	1942-43	Wilmott, Raymond	1940-41-42
		Williams, Eric	1998-99
		Williams, James L.	1974-75-76-77
		Wills, Edward	1934

T

Taggart, Charles	1933-34	Wills, Howard	1933
Taub, Lawrence S. (mgr.)	1968	Wynne, Peter	1982-83
Taylor, Richard W.	1962-63		
Taylor, William	1923		
Thaw, Charles	1953		

Z

Thomas, Etan	1999	Zimmerman, Gifford	1922
Thomas, Jay	1943	Zilumick, Conrad C.	1954
Thompson, Robert (mgr.)	1928	Ziolko, Mark	1971-72
Thompson, Stephen M.	1987-88-89-90		

JIMMY WILLIAMS, LETTERWINNER, 1974-75-76-77

159